PENGUIN CLASSICS

THE MOST VENERABLE BOOK

Nothing at all is known about the authors and compilers of *The Most Venerable Book* (*Shang Shu* – also known as *The Shu Jing: Classic of Chronicles*). It is believed to have been edited by Confucius, but in fact the contents both predate and heavily postdate his life.

MARTIN PALMER has translated a number of key Chinese texts, including *The Book of Chuang Tzu* (Penguin Classics). He is Director of the International Consultancy on Religion, Education and Culture (ICOREC) and Secretary General of the Alliance of Religions and Conservation (ARC). He has written and commentated extensively on Chinese religious traditions. His most recent book is *Sacred Land*.

JAY RAMSAY has collaborated with Martin Palmer on a number of Chinese texts as a poet since 1991. Author of *The White Poem*, *Alchemy*, *Kingdom of the Edge*, *Crucible of Love*, *The Poet in You*, and *Out of Time*, he also works as a psychotherapist in private practice and runs poetry and personal development workshops worldwide. His latest collection is *Monuments*.

VICTORIA FINLAY is the author of *Colour: Travels Through the Paintbox* and *Buried Treasure: Travels Through the Jewel Box*.

T0332960

The Most Venerable Book

Shang Shu

also known as the

Shu Jing
The Classic of Chronicles

Translated by MARTIN PALMER
with JAY RAMSAY and VICTORIA FINLAY

PENGUIN BOOKS

This book is dedicated to Sally Miller, whose arrival
in this world has brought joy to all her family but especially
to her grandfather, Martin.

PENGUIN CLASSICS

Published by the Penguin Group
Penguin Books Ltd, 80 Strand, London WC2R ORL, England
Penguin Group (USA) Inc., 375 Hudson Street, New York, New York 10014, USA
Penguin Group (Canada), 90 Eglinton Avenue East, Suite 700, Toronto, Ontario, Canada M4P 2Y3
(a division of Pearson Penguin Canada Inc.)
Penguin Ireland, 25 St Stephen's Green, Dublin 2, Ireland (a division of Penguin Books Ltd)
Penguin Group (Australia), 707 Collins Street, Melbourne, Victoria 3008, Australia
(a division of Pearson Australia Group Pty Ltd)
Penguin Books India Pvt Ltd, 11 Community Centre, Panchsheel Park, New Delhi – 110 017, India
Penguin Group (NZ), 67 Apollo Drive, Rosedale, Auckland 0632, New Zealand
(a division of Pearson New Zealand Ltd)
Penguin Books (South Africa) (Pty) Ltd, Block D, Rosebank Office Park,
181 Jan Smuts Avenue, Parktown North, Gauteng 2193, South Africa

Penguin Books Ltd, Registered Offices: 80 Strand, London WC2R ORL, England

www.penguin.com

This translation first published in Great Britain by Penguin Classics 2014
010

Translation copyright © Martin Palmer, 2014
Editorial material copyright © Martin Palmer, 2014
'The Poet and the Text' copyright © Jay Ramsay
All rights reserved

The moral right of the translators and author of the editorial material has been asserted

Set in 10.25/12.25 pt Adobe sabon
Typeset by Jouve (UK), Milton Keynes
Printed in Great Britain by Clays Ltd, Elcograf S.p.A.

ISBN: 978-0-141-19746-3

Contents

THE MOST VENERABLE BOOK

The Book of Yu

The Book of Xia

The Book of Shang

The Book of Zhou

Introduction

In the year 213 BC the First Emperor of all China, the notorious Qin Shi Huang Di, whose vast tomb is still guarded by the famous Terracotta Army, issued a decree. He ordered that all books except those dealing with medicine, war, divination or agriculture should be seized. He especially wanted to destroy all evidence that there had ever been a world of ideas, beliefs, values, stories or history before he had seized power eight years previously. He believed that if no one could read about other ways of ruling an empire, then no one would ever challenge him or those who followed him.

He was planning to destroy the books in order to create a dynasty that would last for a thousand years. And he very nearly succeeded. Not in creating the thousand-year dynasty – in fact it lasted just fifteen years, ending in 206 BC, three years after his own death. But he did nearly succeed in destroying all the books. This was a world before printing. All books were handwritten on slips of bamboo tied together, top and bottom, to form scrolls. The strips were hung vertically, which is why traditionally Chinese writing runs from the top to the bottom. Such books were very fragile and if the string broke or rotted there was no easy way of knowing which strip followed which. You needed to work it out from the text itself. Or hope that someone had memorized the text.

At the top of the list for destruction was this book, the *Shang Shu*: a chronicle of great and terrible rulers in the ancient past, and the rise and fall of dynasties and emperors. It means 'the most venerable book'; *shang* being the Chinese word for 'revered' or 'most venerated', and *shu* being Chinese for 'a book'. Its other title is the *Shu Jing*, which is often translated as the *Classic of History* or perhaps more accurately as the *Classic of Chronicles*.

The reason for the First Emperor's particular hatred of this book becomes clear almost as soon as you start to read. Here, on page after page, you meet the heroes of ancient China. Benevolent rulers; sagacious ministers; extraordinary people heroically struggling against floods and against corruption. Here, also, we have those who lay down their lives to try to preserve order and decorum; those who take huge risks to try to reform wayward kings; others who lay out in great detail how a kingdom should be ruled and who remind the ruler that the purpose of kingship is to make the lives of the ordinary people better.

And side by side we have some of the greatest anti-heroes of ancient Chinese history. In the figure of King Zhou, the last ruler of the Shang Dynasty (traditionally said to have died in 1122 BC) we have the epitome of the vicious despot.

While there is considerable controversy about how accurate or authentic these accounts are, nevertheless they do refer to real rulers and events which mostly happened well over three thousand years ago. And thanks largely to this book they are remembered to this day. Figures whom you are about to meet, such as Yu and Yi, King Wen and perhaps particularly the Duke of Zhou, will crop up in everyday conversation in China. They are folk heroes in China; and their behaviour and morality continue to be relevant today.

For China is the oldest continuous culture in the world. Egyptian records and Babylonian records might go back for four or five thousand years, but nobody today actually still venerates the ancient figures of Pharaonic Egypt or the gods of ancient Babylon. But in China, Shun and Yao – two of the Five August Rulers you will meet in this Book – are still revered and respected as founder figures of Chinese civilization.

For Westerners, it is useful to recall that at the time of the overthrow of the Shang Dynasty by the Zhou some three thousand years ago (which is the greatest event in this book), Rome did not yet exist. Greece didn't even have a written language. In Israel, King David was shortly to come to the throne and in Egypt the Twenty-first Dynasty was just commencing. In Britain, the era of stone circles was coming to an end, but of the tribes, their kings and their trials and tribulations we have now not the faintest idea. But China's memory of the past is a continuous one and this is why the *Shang Shu* was – and increasingly today is – so important and why it was such an object of hatred for the First Emperor.

It is worth recalling a more recent figure in Chinese history who also wanted to eradicate all memory and knowledge of the past – knowledge which might challenge his autocratic rule. Chairman Mao launched the Cultural Revolution in 1966 with the explicit aim of destroying all elements of China's 'feudal and imperial past'. In the chaos that was unleashed, any ancient texts, historic buildings, figures such as Confucius or beliefs such as Daoism or Buddhism were to be attacked and destroyed. And Mao explicitly modelled himself on the First Emperor, whom he saw as praiseworthy for his efforts to eradicate the past. Like the First Emperor, records of the past were a prime target for Mao and his followers, who from 1966 to 1976 sought to destroy the past – and they very nearly succeeded. It is from that holocaust of destruction – not just of historical materials but also of millions of people – that China has spent the last few decades recovering. Now there is a hunger for things that were so nearly destroyed and a sense of returning to the classics. And amongst the treasures being re-evaluated are books such as this one, the *Shang Shu*.

The First Emperor ruled with a huge army to enforce his edicts. Between the years 213 and 209 BC, when the Emperor died, the edict banning the books was in full swing. Copies were snatched from scholars and libraries across the land and brought to the capital city. Tradition has it that all the books were burned and the scholars who refused to surrender their copies were buried alive – one lurid account mentions up to seven hundred of them at one time. What may have been more likely is that in a time of persecution the books were seized and collected, but they were actually destroyed when the Qin Dynasty fell in 206 BC. We do know that the Grand Library in the capital was torched by the rebels when they sacked the city. Whatever the truth, to all intents and purposes the *Shang Shu*, along with other key banned texts, seemed to have been wiped off the face of the earth.

What happened to the physical book and its recovery is a whole history in its own right and we will explore that later. It is a fascinating story of archaeological discovery and controversy. But that is not why this book is worth studying in and for itself. As we will see later, by AD 653 the text translated here was accepted as the genuine text for Confucian study and the Imperial Examination system.

What exactly is the Shang Shu and why was it so important?

For over thirteen hundred years (from the seventh to twentieth centuries), the *Shang Shu* was essential reading. Anyone aspiring to a role in the imperial bureaucracy of China had to spend their childhood and teenage years studying it, together with four other classics, *The Book of Songs* (*Shi Jing*); *The Book of Rites* (*Li Jing*); *The Book of Changes* (*Yi Jing*); and *The Book of the Spring and Autumn Annals* (*Chun Qiu Jing*). All of these had been written down, as well as being part of oral history for hundreds of years before the time of Confucius, but they were all once believed to have been edited by the great sage himself.

Confucius, or, to give his proper Chinese name, Kong Fu Zi, lived from 550 to 479 BC. He was a teacher, bureaucrat and in a strange way a reformer who looked to the past for models of virtue. He highlighted figures, such as the Duke of Zhou, whom he felt had behaved in ways leading to correct action and proper rule, and it was upon them that he based a whole philosophy of moral behaviour.

At the heart of his teachings (expounded especially in the collection of his sayings known as *The Analects*) is the concept of the *junzi* – the ideal nobleman or, to use a rather old-fashioned word, gentleman. This is a person of learning, of culture and of the highest moral principles, whose very existence acts as a counterbalance against corruption, greed, cruelty and abuse of power.

Such a person would practise benevolence, would be virtuous, would observe all the appropriate rituals for venerating his ancestors and would be part of and maintain a system of hierarchy which Confucius believed derived from Heaven itself. This hierarchy placed the Emperor as the Son of Heaven below Heaven itself (and to some extent below the ancestors as well) and then power and authority flowed down from him through ministers to the male head of each family and on down to the lowest levels of society. This, for Confucius, was what is at times referred to in the *Shang Shu* as 'The Way (Dao) of Heaven'. Women were always subservient to the dominant male in the structure, hence the traditional Confucian opposition to female rulers. This gender bias in his teachings has led him to be strongly criticized in the past hundred years or so.

Confucius believed, based upon his reading of the ancient Chinese texts and especially the *Shang Shu*, that there had been such model people in the past. As we will see when we enter into the Book itself, his greatest model is the Duke of Zhou but others also served as models, such as Yu the Great, whose selfless service to the people in trying to protect them from the Great Flood of Chinese antiquity is honoured to this day. By stressing that junzi had existed and using texts such as the *Shang Shu* to 'prove' it, Confucius was saying quite explicitly that his ideas were not just nice ideas but could in fact be realized.

It is no longer thought that he edited any of these texts. He certainly commented on them, and his thoughts were collated later into some of the mainstream commentaries which form a major part of the Confucian tradition.

Whatever the truth of his participation, Confucius's association with these Five Classics gave them a status which put them on to an almost biblical level of sacredness and transcendent significance. It gave them a status that made them central to the Imperial Examination system – itself a manifestation of Confucius's idea of the junzi. Every student sitting for the examinations needed to know these books off by heart, and to be able to quote appropriately from them when necessary.

This book in particular was treated as a handbook to government and law for thirteen hundred years, from the seventh century AD to the twentieth.

It was the textbook of Confucian power and yet it is also a deeply subversive book – as we shall discover.

To begin with, it is important to understand the traditional chronology of the book, which changes from section to section.

The earliest chapters, one to nine, are stories from mythological times and the dates traditionally ascribed to them are simply ways of setting the events in some sort of order. There can be no exactness about quasi-mythological figures such as Yao, Shun and Yu. This is made clear in the very first line of the Book. Trying to produce a literal translation, it would be best translated as 'It is said that if we investigate back into antiquity', which I have translated as 'Long, long ago'. It does not try to claim it is a document written at the time nor to say that the events happened at a precise time.

Chapters ten to twenty-four are given traditional dates in order to establish a running order of rulers and events, but they are largely beyond verification. However, when we come to the remainder of the book (chapters twenty-five to fifty-eight), the Zhou invasion and conquest of the Shang, we are on firmer ground. The traditional dates have the fall of the Shang in 1122 BC. Today, whilst there are various alternatives, it is generally accepted that this fall probably took place around 1050 BC. Consequently all dates for the succeeding rulers of the Zhou change by about eighty years. For example, traditionally King Wu reigned from 1122 to 1115 BC as the first ruler of the Zhou dynasty. Modern research would place his reign as between 1046 and 1042 BC. King Cheng, his successor, traditionally reigned from 1115 to 1078 BC and is now thought to have ruled from 1042 to either 1020 or 1005. By the time we get to King Mu, who traditionally reigned from 1001 to 946 BC, it is now thought that he reigned from either 976 to 922 or from 956 to 917 BC. However, to be in accord with the traditional Confucian dates, I have in this book used the traditional (rather than later) dates for each reign.*

The whole book is divided into four sections or Books, reflecting four traditional eras in Chinese history.

The Book of Yu (sometimes called Shun)

This is named after Shun, who is the last of the Five August Rulers of antiquity. It covers the period traditionally from 2357 to 2205 BC. These are chapters one to five.

The Book of Xia

The Xia dynasty is traditionally seen as China's first dynasty. It begins with the foundation of the Xia by Yu the Great and ends with the overthrow of the last king, who is corrupt and evil. The traditional dates are from 2205 to 1766 BC. These are chapters six to nine.

The Book of Shang

This runs from the conquest of the Xia by Tang the Conqueror in 1766 BC to the fall of the Shang dynasty and the overthrow of evil King Zhou, traditionally ascribed to the year 1122 BC. These are chapters ten to twenty-six.

The Book of Zhou

This traditionally runs from the fall of the Shang in 1122 BC to the final documents which are traditionally dated to either the rule of King Ping (770 to 719 BC) or that of King Hsiang (651 to 618). Disagreement about which ruler these final texts (chapters fifty-six and fifty-eight) concerns has been continuous since

* The two sets of alternative dates are based upon the Chinese government's own attempts to finalize a date under what is called the Xia–Shang–Zhou system (which gives 976 to 922 for King Mu) while the second set of dates is based upon the Cambridge University History of China calculations (which gives 956 to 917 for King Mu).

around 100 BC! I have opted for the King Ping dates. These chapters are twenty-seven to fifty-eight.

In introducing each section I have indicated which chapters are thought to be most authentic and which are considered to be later creations or rewrites.

THE BOOK OF YU – 2357 to 2205 BC

Chapters 1 to 5

In chapters one to five (only chapter three is not considered to be genuine and ancient) we encounter many of the core themes of the *Shang Shu*. We also meet three of the greatest semi-mythological rulers of ancient China. They are semi-mythological because there probably were rulers who, in keeping with shamanic practice, combined the roles of both priest and king (see chapter five). They were known as Yao, Shun and Yu the Great. Shamanism and ancestor worship were the two main religious systems of ancient China. Both are reflected in various ways throughout the early chapters. The most startling example of shamanic practice and ancestor veneration is the dramatic conclusion to chapter five, when Kui, advisor to the Emperor Shun, says the following:

'Let us strike the chimes; play the stringed instruments; sing and chant in order to bring the ancestors to visit us. Let us call up the spirit of Yu and all the great leaders of the past.'

With flutes and drums, with rattles and all sorts of other musical instruments, the birds and animals started to dance. At the nine notes, even phoenixes, both male and female, came to dance their stately dances.

Kui noted, 'See how, when the ritual music is played, all of life joins in joyfully and all the leaders of the people are happy.'

This is followed by the Emperor Shun composing and singing a song. This ritual role is often found in shamanic accounts of powerful figures who combine not just kingly rule but also priestly, spiritual roles and powers. This is especially the case when, through music and chant, not just ancestors but also mythical creatures such as the phoenix are summoned.

It is not surprising then that the opening chapters take us beyond the realm of mortals. One of the great epic stories of China is that there was a Great Flood – that the Yellow River burst its banks and wrought devastation across the heartland of the country probably some time in the later third millennium BC, four or five thousand years ago. There are elements of the stories associated with this great disaster throughout the early chapters. In chapter one we are told that:

> ... the ceaseless floods and the vast waters are destroying every-
> thing that is good and right. The dark waters have overwhelmed
> the hills and mountains. They have raged right up to Heaven
> itself while the people below, why, they are in despair.

In the same chapter we hear of Gun, the tragic hero who failed in the task of curbing the flood. 'For nine years Gun struggled, trying to succeed at the task set him, but he failed.' In the next chapter – the Chronicle of Shun – we hear of Gun again (though he is not named). By now he has been exiled to a remote island for having failed to overcome the flood. Here he is called a notorious villain and later in chapter thirty-two – The Great Plan – we hear that he 'upset the Five Elements' and this 'provoked the Ruler to great anger and as a result he did not share with him the Great Plan in its Nine Sections'.

The greatest hero we are introduced to in the early chapters is Yu the Great. Yu was the son of Gun, who succeeded where his father had failed. The stories told about him in popular Chinese culture are full of divine powers and strange events. For example, he rides a dragon, slices through entire mountains and fights demons. To any Chinese reader, such legends lie behind these chapters, though they are not mentioned in this book. The famous stories which we do hear about in these chapters are the ones which tell us that even though he had only been married for three days (chapter five) he left home to battle against the Flood, and that even when his son was born he never returned home. As the Emperor Shun comments in chapter three – The Counsels of Yu the Great – when the Great Flood threatened to overwhelm them, Yu was 'unending in your labours for the country's benefit, barely giving a thought to your own family, your own home'. Yu is the epitome of the Confucian worthy, the selfless servant of the Emperor and of the people.

Beyond the story of the Great Flood, these first chapters introduce us to a number of key ideas which shape the whole book and have as a result shaped China for at least thirteen hundred years – and almost certainly profoundly influenced it for a thousand years before that.

One such key idea, and the one which makes this book so subversive, is the notion of the Mandate of Heaven. While various unnamed deities are mentioned from time to time throughout the book, they are not powerful figures. They tend to be simply referred to as 'the deities of nature' and are linked to rivers and mountains. Or they are occasionally summoned through divination or through a medium. In the earliest chapters there is no reference to a God-type figure. Heaven is spoken of, but only rarely, and while in chapter two we have a term 'Emperor Above', this I think refers to an ancestor such as the founder figure of China, the Yellow Emperor Huang Di, whose mythic powers make him a half-divine, half-human figure. His tomb in Shaanxi province is still venerated to this day as the resting place of the First Ancestor – a term which also appears from time to time in these early chapters.

Instead of a God, what we have is 'Heaven' and Heaven is a force which orders the way of life but which is, at least in these early chapters, unemotional and to a very great degree unconcerned with the intricacies of human life. Instead it is only really interested in the continuation of a balance between Heaven and Earth, which can be disturbed by inappropriate actions of primarily human beings. It lacks almost all the features which other traditions would ascribe to a god or to a hierarchy of deities. (See also below, pages xxx–xxxiii.)

Chapter four gives a very telling account of Heaven:

Heaven, like us, sees clearly and hears clearly. Heaven inspires awe and rewards accordingly and this the people can see clearly. Heaven and Earth, above and below, everything is linked. And as a result, wise men will take their responsibilities within this order very seriously.

As chapter three – The Counsels of Yu the Great – says, 'When Heaven is in control and Earth obedient, then all creation will be in balance; all things will be in harmony.'

Heaven is a cosmic force of order and yet it has one major role in the affairs of humanity. It bestows the right to rule on individuals and through them upon entire dynasties. It also has the power to remove that mandate to rule and bestow it upon another person and dynasty if those who currently hold the mandate fail to live up to the highest standards. In the early chapters, this notion is fairly vague and undeveloped. For example, in chapter two we hear that it was clear Shun had the qualities which meant 'he had the Mandate of Heaven'.

As the book progresses, the Mandate of Heaven becomes a central theme of power and authority. In essence, if the people believe that Heaven has withdrawn its mandate, then it is legitimate to overthrow a ruler and therefore also the dynasty. We shall explore this in more detail later on, but one important point needs to be made here. The right of the people to overthrow a corrupt ruler and dynasty is a political idea which time and time again has shaped the history of China. As recently as 1976, it formed part of the psychological context which inspired the mass movement which overthrew the Gang of Four.* It is of great antiquity and certainly at least as old as the Zhou dynasty, c.1050 BC, if the many references to it in the Book of Zhou section of the *Shang Shu* are anything to go by.

To put this in perspective, in Europe it was only in the twelfth century AD and in the writings of John of Salisbury† that this

---

* See James Palmer, *The Death of Mao*, Faber and Faber, London 2012, p. 64f.
† His position was set forth in his book *Policraticus* and sharpened by his siding with Thomas Becket, the Archbishop of Canterbury, who opposed the abuse of power by King Henry II of England. John was in Canterbury the day Thomas was murdered in the cathedral.

notion of the right of the people to overthrow a corrupt ruler and dynasty was clearly articulated. China has had the notion of regime change built into its very system of political thought for at least two thousand years, probably three thousand years.

Tied in with this notion of the Mandate of Heaven is the central importance of virtue. The character for virtue appears on almost every page of the book. It is the heart of morality and the possession or lack of virtue determines the fate of each person. Virtue is so fundamental to the Confucian worldview that it becomes in effect the code word for being eligible for the Mandate of Heaven. Throughout the book, the need to be virtuous, to act virtuously, is hammered home.

For example, in chapter four, Gaoyao, a model Confucian official, a true junzi, says the following:

> Pondering upon this, Gaoyao said: 'In reality there are the nine virtues and if someone has these, then such a person, in our experience, will always act appropriately.'
>
> 'And what are these?' asked Yu.
>
> Gaoyao replied, 'They are, in sequence:
>
> generosity balanced by discipline
> evenness balanced by resolve
> willingness balanced by respect
> confidence balanced by reverence
> assurance balanced by boldness
> directness balanced by gentleness
> simplicity balanced by discernment
> verve balanced by integrity:
> courage balanced by justice.
>
> 'Anyone with this kind of integrity will always be successful. If three of these virtues shape how you behave day by day, then this will bring enlightenment to everyone in the family. If you conduct yourself day by day with six of these virtues, then the beloved homeland will be well governed. If all nine virtues are the basis of your life, then all will be well for everyone. This is how those

few people in charge of the many will ensure that everything is done in balance with the foundational elements of the universe itself.'

In chapter fifteen, the second part of the Instructions to King Tai Jia, the advisor Yi Yin, another model of Confucian junzi, says the following to the young king:

'If you can really be sincere and virtuous and can follow the will of your ancestors, then you will be a good ruler. The First King cared like a child for the poor and for those who suffered, and as a result the people were happy to obey him – indeed they did so cheerfully. For example, when he was visiting one area, the people in the neighbouring areas would say they couldn't wait for him to visit them, because whenever he visited, injustice would cease.

'Dear King, be virtuous. Model yourself on your worthy ancestor. Do not indulge in negligence but instead, when you reflect upon your ancestors, consider the importance of filial piety. When you give orders to those under you, do so gracefully. When planning for the future, make sure you have clarity of vision. When contemplating virtue, listen carefully. Then I will be able to serve Your Majesty without ceasing.'

These early chapters also introduce us to another aspect of the religious or spiritual life of ancient China: divination. Two main forms of divination are mentioned a number of times, starting with chapter three, where we hear:

Yu said, 'Let me seek advice through divination regarding which are the worthy ministers, and follow its advice.'

The Emperor replied, 'Yu. The Diviner makes his decision first, then he consults the Great Tortoise Shell in order to determine if this is the Will of Heaven. Likewise I make up my mind and only then do I consult with everyone. They then agree that this is what fate decrees and even the deities concur – indeed all the forms of divination agree. When divination gives such a full answer, you don't do it again.'

The tortoise shell was one of the two methods, the other being the use of yarrow sticks.

The tortoise shell or turtle shell was used for divination by having a series of indentations cut or chiselled into the base of the shell. After prayers were said, a heated stick was applied to the indentations on the bottom of the shell, which caused cracks to appear on the top of the shell. The cracks were then read or interpreted as pictures or indications of an answer to the question posed. For example, if the question posed was 'When should we attack?' and a picture of what looked like the moon was discerned in the cracks, this would mean attack at night. At various points in the book we hear what those questions were. In chapter thirty-four, 'The Golden Chest', we hear that the Duke of Zhou sought advice through divination as to whether the king would survive his terrible illness.

It was from these cracks which were interpreted as pictures that Chinese characters and calligraphy arose around 1700 BC. The use of a turtle or tortoise shell was considered the most powerful divination tool as the answer seemed to appear, as it were, from Beyond. In Chinese legend, it was on the shell of a cosmic turtle which was seen by the Original Ancestor, Fu Xi, that the divine pattern of the universe was revealed to humanity. This is referred to in chapter fifty, where amongst the ritual objects set out at the funeral of the king is the River Chart – so called because the turtle crawled out of a river in front of Fu Xi. On the back of the turtle were the trigrams – sets of three lines which were either yin or yang in meaning and from which, according to Chinese mythology, one of the Five Classics the Yi Jing and all associated divination insights and cosmologies developed.

The second method was the use of yarrow sticks, which are also known as 'milfoil'. By casting a set number of sticks, an answer is given. This method has survived because it is used for Yi Jing readings to this day. As we shall see later, the Yi Jing is intricately involved with the later sections of the Shang Shu.

Ancestors have been mentioned above in connection with the shamanic tradition, but they are in and of themselves a major theme throughout the book. Deified ancestors walk through the book from the first mention in chapter two of the First King. We hear of how the Emperor Shun conducted a 'sacrifice to the Noble Ancestor' at the 'Temple of the Ancestors' on his safe return from his tour of inspection. Twice we hear of a victorious new dynasty providing funds and support for the continuation of rituals and sacrifices to the ancestors of the fallen dynasty. For example, as set out in chapter thirty-six, when the most senior survivor of the fallen House of Yin is given this commission:

> The king spoke to the eldest son of the King of Yin and appointed him to oversee the rites and rituals due to his ancestors. He said:
>
> > 'Follow the example of your ancient ones,
> > the virtuous ones,
> > for I can see you are a worthy man
> > like your revered ancestors.
> > Therefore
> > I appoint you to conduct the correct rituals and protect
> >   the relics.
> > You will be a guest in my Household,
> > a friend to the State
> > and this will last for generation after generation.'

Failure to properly honour the ancestors is second only to the failure to honour Heaven in the crime sheet compiled against corrupt rulers. The divine status of the ancestor is spelled out very clearly in chapter thirty-four, when the Duke of Zhou creates a special set of three altars in order to speak directly to the Three Ancestor Kings so that he can plead for the life of the ill king.

In these early chapter we also meet a core Confucian ideal: that of the ruler who moderates punishments in order to inspire moral reformation. While the book contains very detailed instructions about punishments – chapter fifty-five is essentially a legal handbook on the scale of punishments from nose-slitting to execution – the mark of a truly great ruler is his ability to show compassion and restraint. This is set out in chapter two, where Shun is praised because:

He took special interest and care in defining punishments. He ordered that mutilation or execution should be replaced by banishment, that offending officials should be whipped, that scholars who were unworthy should be caned and that fines should be brought in as compensation for crimes. If someone did something wrong by mistake or ignorance, they were to be pardoned, but anyone who abused their power, and did so constantly, was to suffer the most extreme punishment – execution. His watchwords were 'Beware! Beware!' and he attempted to moderate punishment with compassion.

In chapter three the role of the ruler in establishing order through law in order to teach the people how to behave is clearly stated:

Then, turning to Gaoyao, the Emperor said:

> 'Because you are the High Judge, I know that no one, neither my ministers nor my people, will break the law. Using the power of punishment, you have taught the people of all ages to honour and respect the True Law and so everyone is governed well. Because you used restraints, the people no longer need to be made to follow the Middle Path: they just will do so naturally. Just keep on like this.'

The mention of the Middle Path here also brings us to another recurring theme: that of following the Path or Way of Heaven. Confucius was a follower of the Way – the Dao, as it is pronounced in Chinese. We are used to the tradition of Daoism based upon the writings of Lao Zi and Zhuang Zi, but it is often forgotten that Confucius was also in a sense a 'Daoist', a follower of the Way. The difference between the *Shang Shu*/Confucian notion of the Dao and that of the Daoist religion itself is that the *Shang Shu* Dao is the Dao of Heaven – a moral code which must be followed or severe penalties will result. The Daoist notion of the Dao is the Way of Nature, a much more cosmic notion which is about flowing with the streams of consciousness of the universe rather than following a moral code.

When the Dao – Path or Way – is mentioned, as in the quote from chapter three above, it is a moral code that is meant. The context of the quote above from chapter three shows clearly this aspect of the *Shang Shu* understanding of Dao.

Chapter three also introduces us to the Five Elements of Classical Chinese thought. There is much debate about when the notions of the twin opposites, yin and yang, and then of the Five Elements – water, fire, metal, wood and earth – were first developed, and it is on the basis of the inclusion of the Five Elements in chapter three that it is thought to be a third to fourth century AD edited text or possibly, according to some, creation. As Needham points out, the earliest thorough outline of the Five Elements theory comes in the writings of Zou Yan in the fourth century BC.* This is not to say that such ideas were not in circulation prior to this, which would potentially take us back into the last stages of the Zhou dynasty's actual rule.

At various points throughout the book, the regulation of the kingdom is seen as part of an accord with the regulatory forces of nature and of the universe. This is made explicit in this quote from chapter three:

> And bear in mind that true virtue is the basis of good governance, and governance is deemed to be good if it contributes to the well-being of the people. See how the cosmos regulates the Five Elements of water, fire, metal, wood and earth in order that it functions properly. Therefore, uphold virtue and this will increase well-being; support creativity and this will help balance all life . . .

The clear links between the order of the cosmos and the order of human behaviour are once again strongly emphasized here.

The greatest exposition of Classical Chinese philosophy comes in chapter thirty-two – The Great Plan – and probably does date from around the time of Zou Yan. See page 91, below.

Finally, we find within the first few chapters most of the styles of literature which will shape the whole book. These

* Joseph Needham, *Science and Civilisation in China*, Volume II, Cambridge University Press, 1956, p. 232ff.

range from chronicles, such as chapters one and two; through counsels, such as chapters three and four; to speeches, such as chapter seven. Later we also meet announcements, such as chapter eleven; instructions, as in chapter thirteen; and charges, as in chapters twenty-one to twenty-three. In terms of actual style, we range from poetry, as in chapter five; to speeches – found pretty much throughout the book; to reporting, as in chapter six; and prose, in many different places. We also have wisdom sayings, such as this one from chapter three:

A leader should be loved. Who should be feared? *The people.*

The book contains a vivid picture of the diversity of literary styles and of the standard ways of recording 'history' in ancient China. As such, it shares many of these features with other ancient books such as the Old Testament or the *Iliad*.

The Book of Xia

The Book of Xia section of the *Shang Shu* comprises chapters six to nine. This very patchily covers the period of the Xia Dynasty, which traditionally is ascribed to the years 2205 to 1766 BC. Yu the Great reigned from 2205 to 2197 and it is to his reign that chapter six – Yu's Report to Heaven – is dated.

Chapter six is one of the most complex chapters in terms of translation because it is in effect a compendium of place names and geographical, agricultural data from across ancient China. As such, it is a unique account of the China of perhaps three thousand years ago and from it scholars have been able to glean more about the nature of the landscape of ancient China than from any other document. I have translated it here as a bureaucratic report, following the pattern of each section, moving from the name of the region, through its physical description, type of soil and tax return, to the tributes it sends to the capital and the river system which it uses to send the tributes.

This model of a central ruler to whom tribute is sent establishes the pattern for all succeeding imperial systems throughout China's dynastic history. It also, in the extraordinary mapping out of the zones of China at the end of the chapter, establishes the name of China. The Chinese name means the Middle Kingdom – the centre of the universe, in effect – and this sense of the central role of the Chinese Emperor and empire derives its strength in part from this chapter. Unlike ancient Muslim maps, where Makkah is the centre of the world even if the mapmaker lives in Indonesia, or medieval Christian maps, where Jerusalem is the centre even if, as with the Mappa Mundi, the mapmaker lives in Hereford, England, in China, the Emperor and his city are the centre – a point which is made later on in the book, in chapter forty, when the new Zhou dynasty decides to build a new capital.

> By building this great city, he will be seen as a worthy counterpart of the Emperor of Heaven. He will make sacrifices to the spirits in Heaven and on Earth and then he will rule benevolently from this middle place. By the king ruling well and truly honouring and respecting the Mandate, the people will stay happy.

The quite astonishing map of the zones reflects the idea that the further you go away from the Emperor and the Han Chinese, the more barbaric and wild the people become. A notion which still finds a resonance in China today.

The Covenant at Gan – chapter seven – is believed to be one of the oldest documents, and describes a revolt against the next ruler of the Xia dynasty, Yu's son Qi. Qi dies, having suppressed the revolt, in the year 2189.

Chapter eight – the Lament of the Five Sons – is very similar in style to the contemporary book in the Five Classics, the Book of Songs. Through poetry it tells of the overthrow of one of the later Xia rulers, Dai Gong, around the year 2159. He is the first example of a 'bad ruler' and the lament highlights how through his 'outrageous' style of living, 'boozing, dancing and carousing the night away', he has lost the right to rule not least because his ancestors are appalled by his behaviour.

These verses, considered to be part of the later edition or version from the third to fourth century AD, are powerful in the evocation of a dynasty falling apart and the personal tragedy that comes through corruption at the highest level.

The diagram of the Five Tenures

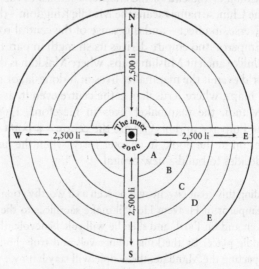

■ The Capital
A. The First Tenure: The Land of Nobles
B. The Second Tenure: The Zone of Security
C. The Third Tenure: The Forbidden Lands
D. The Fourth Tenure: The Barbarian Lands
E. The Fifth Tenure: Where the worst criminals are exiled

The final document of the Xia is chapter nine – the Punishment of Yin – describing events in the reign of Zhong Kang, who ruled between 2159 and 2147 BC. It is thought to be a later chapter from the third to fourth century AD, but it does seem to contain material and information from a much earlier time. The Astrologers Royal, Xi and He – names we met in chapter one and which now seem to have become hereditary titles – have failed in their duties. They failed to predict an eclipse and this caused chaos and distress. But worse than this, it made the ruler look as if he was not privy to the ways of Heaven. It made him look as if Heaven had withdrawn the special relationship by which he had the right to rule. This could have fatally undermined his authority and led to him and his dynasty being overthrown.

The failure to predict eclipses or the occurrence of earthquakes, huge floods or any other natural disaster was seen – indeed is still seen in China – as a sign that Heaven has withdrawn the mandate to rule. Hence the fury of the king and the command to the Prince of Yin to punish Xi and He. It is also clear from the text that Xi and He are in effect challenging the dynasty and this is why an army is sent to enact punishment.

And that is it! We know no more.

Having taken us from 2205 to around 2150 BC, the record of the Xia dynasty misses out the next four centuries and we find ourselves suddenly transported in the next book to the very last Xia ruler and the start of the Shang dynasty.

It is recorded that there were, prior to the First Emperor's ban and the consequential loss of the original full *Shang Shu*, around one hundred chapters of the book. We now have fifty-eight, of which twenty-eight are thought to be from the earliest surviving example – see pages liii–lvii, below. The huge gaps in the Xia chronicle are perhaps indicative of how much was lost.

The Book of Shang

The Shang dynasty – also know as Yin, after their new capital, see chapters eighteen to twenty – traditionally ruled from 1766 to 1122 BC. The Shang chapters are ten to twenty-six. The Shang dynasty was founded by Tang the Conqueror, who becomes, in later Confucian writings, a model ruler.

It is here that for the first time the right of the people to rebel against a corrupt ruler and overthrow not just him but his dynasty is spelled out. In chapter ten, considered to be an early chapter, Tang sets out why he, a ruler of a small region of the kingdom, must overthrow the Xia king:

> But I hear you asking, 'Of what significance is Xia to us?' Well, the king of Xia has brutally oppressed his people and drained their energy. And the people, why, they have lost all hope and they are crying out, begging, 'Is it not time for the sun to die so that we can die also?' So you can see that the ruler of Xia's lack of virtue leaves me with no option but to go ahead and do this.

In chapter eleven, his advisor Zhonghui justifies this act of rebellion by citing the Mandate of Heaven theory, and also by being guided by one of the great Ancestors:

> Let's be frank, the ruler of Xia lost sight of what is virtuous. As a result, the people were living in a state of great fear. This is why Heaven gave our king the courage and the wisdom so he can show the many states of our land how to behave well. He can be guided by the ancient ways of Yu the Great, and therefore he can be worthy of the Mandate of Heaven.

This is made even more explicit in chapter seventeen, when minister Yi Yin says the following when he addresses the king to remind him that he too must be careful not to lose the mandate:

> Heaven is really hard to understand. Its Mandate with a ruler is not a constant one. If the ruler is virtuous and constant, then he will retain his throne. If he is not constant and virtuous, then he will lose everything. The King of Xia was not constant in his virtue. He ignored the spirits and oppressed the people and as a consequence the Heavenly Emperor no longer cared for him. Instead a search was made throughout the land for one upon whom Heaven's Mandate could be bestowed. Someone who was straightforward and virtuous, and who could rule over all the spirits. Both Tang the Conqueror and I, Prince Yin, are straightforward in our virtue and so, when we touched the heart and mind of Heaven, the love of Heaven rewarded us with a clear mandate and we took charge of everything. As a consequence, we had the power to remove the Xia from their control of the world.

In these chapters we also come across a growing sense that Heaven has a ruler, a supreme deity who commands that his representative on Earth, the Emperor – known as the Son of Heaven – act justly. In chapter two we had what I believe is an ancestor who is now worshipped as the Heavenly Emperor, but from now on we begin to hear about a Heavenly Ruler or Ruler on High. This becomes even more prevalent when we come to the Book of Zhou, where we find such terms appearing regularly. Does this mark a developing notion of a heavenly personality?

In chapter eleven we hear about the Supreme Heavenly Sovereign Spirit and in chapter fifteen we hear of the Emperor of Heaven, while in chapter nineteen we read of the Ruler on High. It is clear that in these chapters, Heaven has become a mirror of the imperial system on earth – or as the Confucians would argue, the imperial system mirrors the Heavenly Order – the Heavenly Way.

It has been tempting for some translators to call this figure 'God'. At times James Legge, the first serious translator, does so in his translation of the *Shang Shu*, reflecting both his nineteenth-century missionary background but also his genuine desire that Westerners take the Confucian classics seriously as spiritual texts. He hoped to achieve this in part by using the word 'God' and to some extent by stylistically basing his own translations on the metre and rhythm of the King James version of the Bible (1611). By these means he intended the Western reader to feel that Confucian and Daoist books were potentially as important as the Bible. He was also part of a debate which arose within the missionary community in China (who tended to be the prime movers in taking Chinese culture and literature seriously until the rise of a more scholarly approach in the early twentieth century) about whether the Chinese had been vouchsafed a revelation from God similar to that given to the Israelites in the Old Testament. In other words, did the Chinese receive a special revelation and thus have a special relationship with God along the same lines as ancient Israel? And if so, did this revelation and relationship become confused, lost and obscured by the rise of later religious practices, in the same way as the Old Testament at times presents the Israelites as having lost their way due to 'heathen' practices? Such ideas persist amongst some evangelicals to this day. I was recently asked if the most profound Chinese characters show that they were based upon symbols found in the Book of Genesis. I had to answer that this was not the case.

These considerations lie behind the occasional use of the term 'God' by Legge. I have not used that term because I think it gives a false sense of the nature of what the various Chinese terms mean. If anything, the notion of a 'Ruler on High' reflects a standard of virtue and authority which has to be at the top of the classic model of the universe as envisioned by the Confucian world view. Looking at it anthropologically, a hierarchy which claims that its authority comes from Heaven has to have a Heavenly Ruler who decides that this is so and bestows the Mandate of Heaven. Looked at spiritually, Heaven acts and thus it must have a prime actor who makes things happen. But the sense here is of an instrumental need for a ruler rather than the sense of a personal deity concerned with the well-being of the human realm.

The question of whether such a figure as the Ruler on High or the Heavenly Emperor was the ultimate force of the cosmos was a debate of immense intensity during the period between the end of the Han Dynasty and the rise of the Sui (AD 220 to 589), during which time the *Shang Shu* as we have it today was once again almost completely lost and then reconfigured as a core text (see below). Philosophers such as Wang Bi (AD 226–249) and Gou Xiang (c.AD 252–312) argued in a similar fashion to Aristotle that there has to be an unmoved mover behind everything. Wang Bi puts it thus:

> Things do not struggle among themselves at random. They flow of necessity from their principle of order. They are integrated by a root cause. They are gathered together by a single influence. Thus things are complex but not chaotic. There is multiplicity of them but not confusion.*

Guo Xiang puts it very bluntly:

> Everything that exists moves forward and backward differently, as though there were a True Lord to make them so. But if we search for evidences for such a True Lord, we fail to find any. We should understand that things are all natural and not caused by something else.†

* Quote taken from Joseph Needham, *Science and Civilisation in China*, Volume II, Cambridge University Press, 1956, p. 322.
† Quote taken from Wm Theodore De Bary, Wing-Tsit Chan and Burton Watson (eds), *Sources of Chinese Tradition*, Volume I, Columbia University Press, 1960, p. 242.

This is why we need to be very careful about using terms such as 'God' for phrases such as 'Ruler on High'. There is a greater depth behind the terms than can be captured by simple transposing to the Western concept of God.

Just occasionally, there is a hint of the sort of divine being who listens to the cries of the oppressed people. For example, in chapter twenty-seven King Wu says with regards to why the Shang must be overthrown:

> So, having made sacrifices to the Ruler on High and performed the correct rituals for the deities of the land, I will now lead us all in carrying out the instructions from Heaven. Heaven cares deeply for the people. What the people long for, Heaven means to give. So come now, help me, a simple man, to reform the world.

The sense that comes across from this quote is that the Ruler on High is but an instrument of the Higher Power, which is simply 'Heaven', the unmovable mover.

Into this discussion of Heaven and deities must come the fact that this section in particular shows the role of ancestors who have become divine or at the very least live on and are able to observe what is happening upon Earth, even if their ability to interfere is somewhat unclear. Throughout this section, the role of Tang the Conqueror transcends his purely human life. He becomes the revered and worshipped First King to whom all later rulers have to be held accountable. It is the role of the ancestors to take the place which in Western religious tradition is filled by God, Jesus or the saints and prophets. When in crisis, it is to the ancestors that the noble ministers turn for help.

It is in the Book of Shang that we meet – in full flow of advice and commentary – the fearless and often rather patronizing minister who takes it upon himself to correct and improve the morality of the ruler. The importance of virtue rises to the fore with the Shang dynasty because its eventual dramatic fall is accounted for by the failure of the dynasty to continue to practise virtue.

This is not through lack of ministers and advisors telling the ruler to be virtuous. For example, chapters thirteen to sixteen introduce us to Yi Yin, the chief minister of the ruler who was the grandson and successor of Tang the Conqueror and ruled from 1753 to 1720 BC. In chapter thirteen, Yi Yin sets out very clearly why the practice of virtue and following the Way of Heaven are vital:

> In the past the Xia started off by being worthy, so as a result no wrath descended upon them from Heaven. The spirits of the land and waters were at peace and all life on earth was united – all creatures. However, their descendants did not follow this model, and as a result the Emperor of Heaven sent disasters upon them, through our ruler whom Heaven chose to endow with its Mandate . . .
>
> Now then, arising from such reward for virtue, everything hangs on how you all begin. Start by showing true affection to your own family because if you can show it to them, then you can go on to show it to the State and then to everyone within the boundaries of our land.

What is very interesting in the midst of the sagacious advice offered is the political insight and indeed wisdom. The Confucian ethic – or perhaps this is better termed ethos – often meant that loyal ministers and officials had to be willing to confront corruption at the highest level. Although they were the loyal bureaucracy, they were also expected to be the fiercest defenders of justice, benevolence and virtue. They took upon themselves to correct rulers in order to defend the ordinary people and the seeds of this virtuous opposition are sown here in these chapters.

For example, listening again to Yi Yin, this time from chapter sixteen, which is considered a later possible third- to fourth-century AD text but seems to reflect an ancient tradition of this virtuous minister, he says:

> Come now, my king. As you know, Heaven does not have favourites. It simply rewards those who are respectful. It is the same with the people. They are not uncritical in their affection because they look to see who is really benevolent. The gods don't just accept any offering made to them. They only accept those offered with real sincerity. As you know, it's not easy to sit on the throne Heaven bestows.

> Where virtue is, order is there too.
> Where virtue isn't – chaos.
> Follow the design of order and all will go well.
> Ignore it and it will end in disaster.
> A wise ruler is constantly thoughtful in what he follows.

However, perhaps the greatest hero ministers have to be the Viscount of Wei, brother to the last and most evil king of the Shang dynasty, and the Principal Scholar of the last king of the Shang. The Viscount of Wei lays into the corruption of his brother and the corruption of the vast majority of the scholars, ministers and officials in chapter twenty-six, the very last Shang chapter.

The Viscount was outspoken, and said:

> 'Scholars, great and small, this Yin dynasty
> has now lost its right to rule over our land.
> Our ancestors were appointed from on high
> knowing what needed to be done, and how to do it.
> But all that's been lost through drunkenness,
> and the virtue of the past has been betrayed.
>
> The people of Yin think it's fine
> to perform crimes of daylight robbery and viciousness
> no matter how great or small.
> The nobles even encourage each other in this
> and no one is ever challenged! But now
> the common people are in revolt, and at last
> the whole edifice is collapsing . . .'

In true Confucian style, the Principal Scholar points to the impact of such corruption on the ordinary people when he says 'Look at the poor, they've given up all hope of salvation.'

But it is the final two sentences of his speech in chapter twenty-six which show the virtue of this great man. While others are getting ready to flee, seeking refuge wherever they can, he says:

> We each have to make our own decision,
> and we'll each have to answer for this to our ancestors,
> but I have chosen to stay. My refuge is here.

As the counterpart to the virtuous minister we also meet the king who wants to be virtuous, to be worthy of Heaven's Mandate and who seeks guidance from a virtuous minister. In chapters twenty-one to twenty-three we meet King Wu Ding and his advisor Yue, whom the king sees in a dream and sends out servants to find. Here the king echoes the concern of the sagacious ministers by saying:

> Every morning, every evening
> tell me what you think so I can act virtuously.
>
> If I'm like hard metal
> then you will be my grindstone
> on which I find my edge.
>
> If I'm like one trying to cross a great river
> then you will be my boat I'm rowing across.
>
> If I am like a dry and thirsty land
> then you will be rain to me!
>
> Being honest you will make me so.
> Be like a medicine, which, bitter as it is
> is healing for the patient.
>
> I am a man walking barefoot,
> I need to tread carefully or my feet will be hurt.

This section also contains the three chapters related to the moving of the Shang dynasty capital to a new site known as Yin (close to Anyang City in Henan Province – rediscovered in the late nineteenth century and the site of the first major discovery of oracle bones with early Chinese characters cut into them), which give the Shang the alternative dynastic name, Yin.

Chapters eighteen to twenty tell of King Pan Geng's attempts to persuade his somewhat reluctant people to move. The tone is splendidly tetchy at times, as, for example, in this section from chapter eighteen where he rounds on the moaning, grumbling officials and tries to get them to see that they are all part of something much bigger:

> But now, you are all kicking up a great fuss, making false and pointless claims, and I honestly have no idea what you are all going on about. It is not that I have given up on virtue, but you don't give me any respect. It's as if you cannot see me for who I really am, a straightforward man – as if you are looking at me by the faint light of an open fire. I fear that, through my lack of experience, I am to blame for this. After all, a fishing net only works if all the many strands are in place and holding together. Likewise, a farmer who puts time and trouble into managing his fields will get a good harvest as a result. If you can banish selfishness, then you will help the people and indeed your own family and friends as well.

However, the absolute power he also wields is made quite clear at the end of the chapter when he says, 'Because if you don't [move to the new capital], you will be punished. And then it will be too late to repent.'

The penultimate chapter in this Book of Shang foreshadows the downfall of the Shang through the venal corruption of the last Shang ruler, Zhou. Chapter twenty-five, where minister Zu Yi is confronting the ruler Zhou, ends thus:

> How can you claim to still have the Mandate of Heaven when your manifold wickednesses are only too well known? Very soon the Dynasty of Yin will fall and you will be to blame. Can you not consider the significance of this condemnation and its impact upon your country?

As we saw earlier, in chapter twenty-six all hope has been lost and so we come to the final Book of the *Shang Shu* and the story of the next dynasty, the Zhou, in The Book of Zhou.

The Book of Zhou

From chapter twenty-seven to chapter fifty-eight we have the story of the conquest of the Shang by the Zhou and the establishment of the Zhou dynasty. The Zhou dynasty ruled in theory from 1122 BC (or from 1046 BC according to modern dating systems) to 221 BC. I say in theory because effectively after 770 and a major invasion from the West, it ruled only a part of Eastern China and then from 476 BC only in name as China split into a range of smaller kingdoms. It was the First Emperor who would in 221 BC finally extinguish all the other kingdoms through conquest and create a united China and finally put to rest any notion of the Zhou Dynasty still existing. He founded his own Qin Dynasty instead. Our texts take us to the reign of King Ping who came to the throne in 770 BC.

The Book of Zhou occupies more than half of the total book and with a few exceptions (see below) consists of documents which are considered to be from the oldest version of the book. The Zhou recorded in detail their times and alongside this section of the book we can place another two of the Five Classics, the *Yi Jing* (Classic of Change) and the *Shi Jing* (Classic of Poetry). Both books in very different ways recount the events and processes involved in the overthrow of the Shang by the Zhou. It is possible that both were recited annually alongside the *Shang Shu* at a celebration ceremony where, through drama, liturgy and recitation, the story of the triumph of the Zhou over the corrupt Shang was enacted. The *Li Jing* (Classic of Rites) makes mention of just such a ceremonial retelling. It was similar in a way to the role of Passover plays in Judaism or a Passion Play in Christianity.

The Zhou section opens with the Great Vow, chapters twenty-seven to twenty-nine. Here King Wu of the Zhou announces that he has been commanded by Heaven to overthrow Zhou the Shang ruler. We are traditionally in the year 1123 and Wu outlines in these chapters the terrible crimes of King Zhou. King Zhou is the archetype of the evil ruler and his crimes are known to this day. In these chapters they are simply mentioned in passing. To understand the revulsion with which this evil king has been viewed throughout Chinese history it is useful to know a little more about these infamous incidents. In chapter twenty-seven we read this:

> He has become so lost in drink and lust that he has become a terrible tyrant. He has punished entire families, not just the actual criminal; he has favoured a few families by making key posts hereditary and his obsession with building himself luxurious palaces, vast pleasure complexes with lakes and water features, has been at the expense of you, the people. He has tortured the most loyal and good people and has cut open the bellies of pregnant women.

He was renowned as a drunkard, as promoting only his cronies and for experiments. Here the reference is to his experiments to see how babies grew by ordering that pregnant women have their bellies slit open so that he could see what stage the foetus had reached. He is also infamous for two other experiments on living people which are mentioned in chapter twenty-nine:

> Listen: he dissected the bare legs
> of those who work deep in the paddy fields
> and cut out for casual inspection
> the hearts of the highest men!

It is said that one day, travelling through the countryside in winter, he saw peasants working up to their thighs in cold water planting out the rice. Convinced they must have special legs which could withstand the cold, he had them seized and their legs amputated so he could examine them and compare them with other people, also seized and also cut up in this barbaric way.

Likewise, he wanted to find out if the hearts of virtuous men were different from those of ordinary men. So he had the hearts of some of the wisest and most virtuous men in the land cut out of their bodies to be examined.

On top of this he oppressed the people so that they cried out to Heaven for rescue and he failed to perform the rituals for the veneration of his ancestors.

This is why, as King Wu says, 'The sheer scale of Shang's wickedness is overwhelming and Heaven's Mandate has been given to us so we can destroy them.' In a series of Calls to Action, King Wu summons the people, their leaders and their armies to join him in seeking to overthrow King Zhou.

In chapter thirty we have a dramatic (literally) presentation of the Call to Arms in the Vow at Mu. The armies are about to cross the river and therefore formally invade the Shang. The remarkable thing is that we have a parallel and contemporary account of this invasion by the Zhou, contained in the *Yi Jing* and in the *Shi Jing*. The testimony of both the other books to the historicity of this invasion is important as for the first time we have other documents which corroborate the *Shang Shu* accounts.

Of these, the most significant is the account in the *Yi Jing*. The *Yi Jing* is a set of oracle readings taken in preparation for this invasion and which guided it. These oracles were given over a short period of time. They tell the story of the epic struggle and uprising of the Zhou, which led to the overthrow of the Shang dynasty. Running through the ancient texts of the *Yi Jing* and in the Book of Zhou of the *Shang Shu* is an epic which ranks alongside the Exodus or the siege of Troy. These oracles are also commented upon in the *Shi Jing*. For example:

> Clear and glittering bright
> Are the ordinances of King Wen.
> He founded the sacrifices
> That in the end gave victory
> That are the happy omens of Chou.*

The *Yi Jing* is made up of sixty-four sets of hexagrams – sets of six lines which are either yin, a broken line, or yang, an

---

* Poem no. 216 from *The Book of Songs*, translated by Arthur Waley, first published 1937.

unbroken line – which together, through complex processes, reveal the oracle. Their pattern derives from the River Chart discussed earlier. This cosmic map of relationships was revealed, according to Chinese mythology, to the first being who created life, Fu Xi, on the back of a turtle (see page xxii above). Deeply mysterious, the sixty-four hexagrams are in fact a collection of oracles which inspired faith in the great venture of overthrowing the Shang.

The phrase 'cross the great river' appears seven times in the *Yi Jing*. For the Zhou, living west of the Yellow River, the 'great river' is none other than the Yellow River itself. This vast river was both a physical barrier with the Shang empire and a mental barrier. To cross the great river meant to break out of the mountains and on to the fertile plains. Thus 'crossing the great river' means to undertake a vast enterprise – the conquest of Shang, no less.

Alongside this clue were the various oracles which speak of the difficulties of forging some sort of an alliance – texts such as Hexagram 2, which talks of having 'friends in the South West and losing friends in the North East', or Hexagram 11, in which the 'lesser ones leave and the great come'; only to be followed in Hexagram 12 with 'the great leave and the lesser ones come'. This echoes the following section of chapter thirty in the *Shang Shu*:

'My liege lords, ministers and officials; commanders of the hosts; commanders of the cavalry; commanders of the infantry; leaders of thousands and officers of hundreds,' he said to them all in welcome. 'You have come, all of you, from so many different regions and places. All of you raise your weapons of war and raise your shields as I declare this vow.'

It is also clear that the *Yi Jing* builds up to a climax of expectation around Hexagram 30, traditionally the last hexagram in section one of the *Yi Jing*. Thereafter, the oracles deal not so much with some vast undertaking which everyone has to be drawn into but with the aftermath or consequences of the success of such an undertaking. This too is reflected in the later part of the Book of Zhou in the *Shang Shu*.

The *Yi Jing* provides us with another take on this momentous moment in Chinese history. The hexagrams actually spell out a storyline, though not in conventional fashion, for they were, after all, oracle readings which in many cases forecast or encouraged actions which then followed. What they do is record the progression of thinking and thus of questions to the oracle with regards to how to plan and execute such a major undertaking as the invasion of the Shang dynasty by the Zhou tribes. The reason these oracles were collected together, and were known for some 800 years or so as the 'Changes of Zhou', is quite simply that they are the oracles which led the Zhou to rise against oppression. They are in effect a sort of Bayeux Tapestry of China in words – or the Story of the Exodus for Judaism, which still to this day Jews recite and relive every Passover.

Furthermore, this extraordinary text not only chronicles the invasion but also deals with the problems which then beset the victorious army and people, and ends by posing questions of power and corruption in ways not dissimilar to Greek tragedy or the spirit of the *Iliad*.

The Zhou celebrated their victory over the Shang once a year at their ancestral temple. Ritual dances re-enacted the conquest and it would seem fair to speculate that the oracles associated with the invasion were also annually recalled and recited, leading to the compilation of at least part of what we now know as the *Yi Jing*. This would also have been a likely setting for the retelling of the story in the form we have in the *Shang Shu* itself. This is very similar to the role that some of the Psalms had when they were used to celebrate Israel's victories and conquest and were annually recited in the Temple, or the Celtic, Anglo-Saxon and Norse tradition of bards composing epic sagas to be sung at feasts, recalling the triumphs of the warriors.

Again, in the *Shi Jing* we find this echoed. For example, Poem 226 in Waley's translation (*op. cit.*) is very clear:

> Oh, great were you, King Wu!
> None so doughty in glorious deeds.
> A strong toiler was King Wen;
> Well he opened up the way for those that followed him.
> As heir Wu received it,
> Conquered the Yin, utterly destroying them.
> Firmly founded were his works.

One of the crimes of which Zhou was guilty was the imprisonment of King Wen of the Zhou, father of King Wu. This venerable old man was locked up for over a year. According to later legend, while he was a prisoner in the Shang dungeons he fell to writing down the sixty-four basic texts – 'oracles' – of the *Yi Jing*. Clearly this was not the case. Legend, however, wanted to honour him, for he was the father of the eventual victor over Zhou, and this was one way of doing it.

King Wen was eventually released after he had offered up most of his lands to Zhou in return not just for his own freedom but for agreement from Zhou that a particularly barbaric torture he had invented be abandoned. This torture was known as the 'Grill Roast Technique', where people were laid on red-hot grids and literally cooked alive.

Soon after his return to the Zhou tribes, King Wen died and his son King Wu ascended the throne. He was very different sort of character. Aggressive and opportunist, he soon saw that the Shang dynasty was ready to fall. It was he who called for the oracles to be read for advice on whether to attack or not, and he dominates the opening sections of the Book of Zhou in the *Shang Shu*. It is worth looking briefly at how the *Yi Jing* texts spell out the initial stages of the conquest, for these are echoed in the *Shang Shu*.

The opening text of the *Yi Jing*, Hexagram 1, relates to the offering of an original sacrifice, a mighty immolation which brought 'a favourable oracle'. Here is recorded King Wu's initial sacrifice or offering, seeking advice on whether to even start such a scheme as the invasion of Shang. He was obviously pleased with the positive response.

Hexagram 2 repeats the details of the successful offering and favourable reading, but then expands a bit more into giving a good outline of the sorts of problems that the king has to face. It talks of taking initiatives and of how some of these will fail. It urges perseverance until the right way has been found. It also cautions that not all those who will be invited to join the attack will come. It is a wise piece of advice to a leader preparing for a major undertaking.

The wise advice is continued in Hexagram 3, where again the original successful oracle is repeated. This is followed by cautionary advice.

Hexagram 4 introduces us to something very different. Here, in an extraordinary reading, we have not a third-person voice but first person. The oracle speaks in terms of 'I' – and is obviously becoming frustrated! It rebukes those who keep coming to it and who are youthful and shallow. It would appear that the young leader Wu has been pushing it a bit. The strange oracle has a tremendous ring of authenticity about it. You can see the shaman and the oracle getting fed up with the constant requests for more and more favourable readings. The oracle is basically saying, 'Look, I've said it will work, so stop asking about that and get on with it!' In other words, Wu has now been told most definitely that the oracle is on his side, but that he, Wu, must now seize the moment.

Finally, in Hexagram 5, Wu is given the reading he has been looking for. He is told that if he is confident and makes the right sacrifices, then he can cross the great river. This is the first time the Yellow River is mentioned and given its role as the most serious physical barrier between the two countries. It is clear that when Wu is told to cross the river he is being given authority from Heaven to invade. With this oracle, the conquest is under way. This crossing of the river is narrated in chapter thirty-one of the *Shang Shu*:

> By the Wu Wu*day the army had crossed the ford of Meng and by the next day we were assembled on the borders of Shang in accordance with Heaven's Decree.

* Chinese days are named after a sixty-day cycle, based on the sixty-year cycle of Chinese astrology.

The somewhat confused state of the *Shang Shu* is reflected in the fact that later in the book we have further accounts of the launch of the war – for example, in chapter thirty-five the whole saga is told again.

After the successful conquest, the Book of Zhou chapters constantly refer back to why it was legitimate to overthrow the Shang and they also warn against complacency. For example, in chapter forty the young king is told:

> In the beginning Heaven guided the Yin and their descendants were blessed because they lived in accord with the Mandate of Heaven. But their descendants later squandered everything.
>
> Now our young king has ascended to the Throne. He must not neglect the elders and those people who have true experience, otherwise how will he come to understand the virtue of the ancient ones who themselves were guided by Heaven. Indeed, the king may be just a youth, but he is the chosen son who is expected to unite the ordinary people. He must be always alert to the dangers that confront the people; he must not fail to do this.

Was this why the drama of the conquest was re-enacted each year? To act as a reminder that only constant vigilance could preserve a dynasty from slipping into corruption? It seems likely.

This Book also contains some themes we have explored earlier. For example, the Viscount of Wei whom we met in chapter twenty-six taking his principled stand against the last Shang king, reappears in chapter thirty-six in what may be a later text. Because of his manifest virtue, he is given responsibility by the victorious Zhou for continuing the ritual sacrifices to the worthy former kings of the Shang.

It is in this Book of Zhou that we meet the model *par excellence* of the just, moral and humble Confucian minister: the Duke of Zhou. From the very first time we meet him in chapter thirty-four, we know he is going to be outstanding. His loyalty to the ruling house and his desire to be as anonymous as possible while offering his own life if it can save the life of the sick king are wonderfully told in this chapter, as are the plots against him. When at last the king discovers how loyal and humble the duke has been, he say this, which sums up the pivotal role of the Duke of Zhou as the model minister:

> Holding the Record, the king wept and said, 'We need no further divination for us to understand how dedicated the Duke of Zhou is to the well-being of our Royal House. But because of our foolishness and youth, we did not understand this until today. This explains why Heaven has manifested its anger, so we will discover the true virtue of the Duke of Zhou. Now it is time for me, a mere stripling, to go and meet him, for this is how things should be done in both my Household and my kingdom.'

The worthiness of the Duke of Zhou and the real affection in which he seems to have been held by the people is reflected in the *Shi Jing*. Poem no. 232 in the Waley translation has a constant refrain about when the Duke of Zhou has come to the East (as the ruler of the Lu region):

> Throughout the kingdoms all is well.
> He has shown compassion to us people,
> He has greatly helped us.

A central role of the Duke of Zhou is planning for, finding and helping to build and organize a new capital. The moving of capitals as we saw in the Book of Shang was a complex issue but also a way of making a clean break. Chapters thirty-seven and forty to forty-two concern the creation of the new capital at Luo – now known as Luoyang. They echo many of the themes outlined in the creation of the Shang capital at Yin – people not wanting to go; creating new traditions and structures; divining where best to build the city and so forth.

In between all this we have some extraordinary chapters. For example, chapter thirty-eight is a passionate plea for sobriety amongst officials who have been using the excuse of ritual and formal banquets to get drunk. Not just drunk, but drunk on money set aside for the proper performance of ritual and entertainment. This is a problem which bedevils China to this day, often attacked by leaders such as President Xi, who in 2012 spoke out about this, using astonishingly similar words to those of chapter thirty-eight.

But it is chapter thirty-two which is perhaps, along with chapter fifty, the most fascinating. In chapter thirty-two, the Great Plan, we have a detailed outline of the core elements of ancient Chinese philosophy. This is probably the earliest such clear outline, and even if not all of it comes from the earliest texts, nevertheless it captures the earliest thinking of Chinese cosmology based on the Five Elements concept.

In this chapter we are introduced to the essential tabulations that underpin the Chinese cosmological worldview. There are nine different subsets and even their titles are intriguing:

> The Viscount of Qi replied, 'Long ago, so I have heard, when Gun fought the Great Flood he upset the Five Elements. This provoked the Ruler to great anger and as a result he did not share with him the Great Plan in its Nine Sections. Because of this, the fundamental principles were lost and Gun was forced into exile, where he died. It fell to Yu to rise up and take on the mantle of his task, whereupon Heaven shared with Yu the Great Plan and its Nine Sections.
>
> 'And so it was that everything was once again in order.
>
> 'The first of the Nine is the Five Elements
> the second is respect for the Five Conducts
> the third is taking care of the Eight Regulations
> the fourth is details of the Annual Records
> the fifth is perfecting Princely Rule
> the sixth is proper use of the Three Virtues
> the seventh . . . the Exploration of Uncertainty
> the eighth, the purposeful use of Understanding
> the ninth the careful use of the Five Good Fortunes
> – with a respect for the Six Extremes.'

The Exploration of Uncertainty is my personal favourite. It echoes the final two hexagrams of the *Yi Jing*. These are titled 'No 63 – Finished' and 'No 64 – Unfinished'.

The chapter spells out what each of these sets are, and their meaning, in what can only be considered a synopsis of Chinese philosophy from around 2000 years ago, if not older. As such, it is of immense significance as an insight into the development of core ideas within Chinese cosmology and their relationship to humanity on earth. In the classic Chinese cosmological view, there are three main forces: Heaven, Earth and Humanity. Between them, they are in charge of all life and if any are out of kilter then the cosmos is out of kilter.

This is captured in a quote from the Doctrine of the Mean, written by Confucius's grandson *c.* fourth century BC:

Only those who are the most sincere [authentic, true and real] can fully realize their own nature. If they can fully realize their own nature, they can fully realize human nature. If they can fully realize human nature, they can fully realize the nature of things.

If they can fully realize the nature of things, they can take part in the transforming and nourishing process of Heaven and Earth. If they can take part in the transforming and nourishing process of Heaven and Earth, they can form a trinity with Heaven and Earth.*

The correlation between, for example, the Five Elements (water, fire, wood, metal and earth) and the Five Conducts, which then leads to the Eight Regulations, shows this clearly. One could say, 'on earth as it is in heaven', to quote from the Lord's Prayer.

Chapter fifty (and flowing over into chapter fifty-one) is a detailed description which has the ring of authenticity and may well be one of the oldest documents to have survived. It recounts in great detail the funeral for a king and the coronation of the new king. Here we have a fulsome ritual description of the conduct of a royal funeral and the passing on of power from one ruler to his heir. The chapter is filled with extraordinary detail such as the ritual clothes that the key participants wore; the official layout of the palace; the different roles the

---

* Quote taken from the Confucian Statement on Ecology 2013, Beijing, edited by Professor Tu Wai Ming.

key players had and the sacred objects of ancient China. It is here that we hear about the ritual objects of ancient China such as the River Chart from which the *Yi Jing* comes; the Great Tortoise Divination Shell; the Red Knife; the Great Book of Instructions; the Grand Jade Disc of Fortune and the Heavenly Chime stone. Some of these objects – such as the River Chart – we still know to this day. Likewise, the divination shells which have been excavated from the Shang dynasty sites over the last century or more. In many museums we can look at jade discs and understand that they were symbols of power and authority and Heavenly chime stones are also to be found. But quite what the Red Knife was, or the Book of Instructions, we have no idea.

On a more sinister level, chapter fifty-five takes us in detail into the penal codes of the Zhou. Here, however, the severity (to a modern ear) of what should be done is once again mitigated by compassion – the sign of a truly virtuous ruler.

> 'When both parties are present and ready,
> the judge should listen to the Five Charges.
> If the Five Charges lead to the Five Punishments,
> then so be it.
> If however they do not justify them,
> then don't use the Five Punishments.
> Instead use the lesser ones,
> the Five Penalties . . .
>
> 'Make the punishment fit the crime.
> 'Judge carefully and equitably.'

The chapter sets out the scale of punishments:

> 'If you are uncertain whether to brand someone, commute this to a fine of six hundred ounces of copper – but only when you are sure.
> 'If in doubt about a nose slitting, commute to twice that, but only once you are sure.
> 'If in doubt about a foot amputation, commute this to three thousand ounces of copper, but only once you are sure.

'If in doubt about castration, commute this to three thousand
six hundred ounces of copper, but only once you are sure.

'If in doubt about execution, commute this to six thousand
ounces of copper, but only once you are sure.

The role of justice is to protect the people and to create harmony. This overriding concern means that while there are
severe punishments, the purpose of them is to restore law and
order for the betterment of all.

Finally we come to chapter fifty-eight. And here, frankly, we
have the whole purpose of the *Shang Shu* summed up in two
lines. Through all the ups and down that the *Shang Shu* records,
for a period stretching over nearly two thousand years, this is
what lies at the heart of the whole venture:

> A state can be brought down by just one man.
> It can also rise to glory, because of one man.

Which brings us back to the issue of what happened when one
man, the First Emperor, rose to glory and then brought it all
down again.

The Story of the Book

Our main source for the accounts of book-burning and
scholar-burying comes from the historian Sima Qian (*c.*145–
86 BC), who makes clear his dislike of the First Emperor. The
dramatic accounts of the scale of the persecution of Confucian
scholars and destruction of the books under the First Emperor
make for fascinating reading and have passed firmly into Chinese history and mythology. In recent years other versions of
what happened have been put forward. For example, Mark
Edward Lewis in *The Early Chinese Empires – Qin and Han**
argues that what the First Emperor did was somewhat different.

---

* Mark Edward Lewis, *The Early Chinese Empires–Qin and Han*, History of
Imperial China series, The Belknap Press of Harvard University Press, Cambridge, Massachusetts, 2007.

He says the First Emperor forbade any private individual or group to have copies of the forbidden books and he collected them all together and kept them effectively under lock and key in the Imperial Library of the Academy founded under the First Emperor. Here, they could be studied under strict government control. The destruction of this sole collection of the books was a result of the burning of the capital during the wars which led to the rise of the Han, c.206 BC.

There is a rather fine irony in the fact that there are various stories about what happened in the past to the Classic of Chronicles!

In our journey through the *Shang Shu* above, I have explored the Book as it would have been seen by generations of Confucian students and indeed most scholars – as a coherent text consisting of ancient accounts of the great and the good and the not so good.

But is this Book authentic?

Today we find it almost impossible to enter a world where ancient documents were treated as authentic accounts of the time. We know too much about oral history; about the way ancient authors would lay claim to a great figure of the past to give credibility to their own thoughts and writings. For example, the Five Books of Moses in the Hebrew Bible (Old Testament) are supposed to have been written by Moses himself. Yet they record his death. The creation of 'histories' or 'chronicles' which purport to tell the origins of a people but which were fabricated long after the events they are supposed to narrate can be seen in the *Aeneid* of Virgil and the *History of the Kings of Britain* by Geoffrey of Monmouth. Virgil creates an entire saga of events from the Fall of Troy c.1000 BC down to the foundation of the city of Rome based upon a legendary figure, a grandson of the last king of Troy. This saga gave the emerging Roman Empire (Virgil was writing in the last half of the first century BC) a pedigree for the Classical world and a natural excuse for considering the Greeks (who of course conquered Troy by deception) as inferior and untrustworthy. A similar exercise in justifying a sense of special if not actually divine favour was sought by the Norman kings who in the eleventh to twelfth centuries were conquering lands from France and England to the Holy Land. This was provided by the very imaginative writer Geoffrey of Monmouth, who around AD 1120 wrote his *History*, a book which gave the British in particular a very special sense of also being descended from Troy.

Shakespeare in his Histories has provided for many people the abiding images of the Wars of the Roses and in particular the image of Richard III as a tyrant. Shakespeare was in many ways a propagandist for the Tudors who had come to power by overthrowing Richard III. The great speeches of Shakespeare's Histories, such as Henry V before Agincourt, have become the staple of what we imagine heroic kings to be and say. Yet these are the inventions of a playwright, written down up to two hundred years later. Their power is not to be denied, nor their insights into human nature. But we don't think they are 'authentic' just because they were written down some centuries ago.

The telling of tall stories in order to boost a national or cultural sense of superiority is not unknown today. In the 1960s, for example, Chairman Mao made up the (untrue) story that the only human-constructed edifice on the earth that could be seen by the naked eye from the moon was the Great Wall of China. He did this because his two greatest enemies, the USSR and the USA, were flying into space and clearly were going to land on the moon very soon.

As we shall see in a moment, the authenticity of the various chapters has been challenged for over a thousand years. However, I think that this notion of authenticity is based upon a false assumption of what is authentic and what is not. No one was writing down exactly what was said or done during the Book of Yu's era. Nor, probably, during the Book of Xia era.

Was someone supposed to have sat down as King Wu launched his campaign and gave his great speech (chapters twenty-seven to twenty-nine)? Almost certainly not, so it was obviously constructed afterwards. Some chapters probably are exact records, such as chapter fifty, describing the funeral and the enthronement of the new king some time around 1000 BC. Other documents are accounts of the time, such as the Penal Codes and the Prince of Lu – chapter fifty-five. They do not depend for their authenticity on having been written at a specific time, but do seem to reflect values and attitudes commensurate with their supposed era.

Even those chapters which are most regularly held up as forgeries of the third to fourth century AD probably contain within them shards of earlier texts, possibly even reworkings of poems that were known to be of the time or even about the specific event. For example, some of the chapters, such as chapter thirty-one, give very exact days, months and years – even telling us what stage the moon was at. This echoes the style of the Shang and Zhou bronzes, which often have an inscription giving the precise date and person for whom a vessel was made, where and why. These bronze inscriptions are contemporary with the events they describe and were known to later dynasties. Did the compilers of the chapters, when they sought to restore damaged or lost texts, turn to these records?

Just to dismiss the various chapters as not having been written down at the exact time of the events they report is to fall into a trap of historical literalism, which frankly we now know is irrelevant. It certainly makes sense to try to discern what might reflect accurately attitudes, events and passions of the time, but to dismiss anything that shows signs of being finally composed years, even centuries, later is to demand of this Book a fundamentalism which does no credit to anyone nor to the integrity of the Book itself. It is, after all, a composition created over time by many hands. It is the same as the Bible, which is not the exact words of God dictated to someone at each historic event but a collection of works from different times by different hands which tells us as much about ourselves as it does about the events of history.

The Rediscovery of the *Shang Shu*

The edict of the First Emperor banning books such as the *Shang Shu* was not lifted until well into the next century, around 180 BC, under the new dynasty, the Han. This means that at least in theory, knowledge of the ancient forbidden books was still a criminal offence.

Regardless of how severe or not the prohibition on private

ownership of the forbidden books was, certain Confucian scholars hid their own copies of the books. In more than one case they
did so by hollowing out the walls in their houses, hiding the
books in the gap and then replastering the walls. So powerful is
this story in China, it led to imitation millennia later. When Mao
launched the Cultural Revolution in 1966, his fanatical young
followers, the Red Guard, saw any object from the past as a sign
that the owners or family were counter-revolutionary. Owning a
family photo album showing life before Communism; having any
antique; owning any books other than the works of Mao himself;
owning records of pre-revolutionary music or, even worse, Western music – all these and many others were all denounced; and to
be found in possession of any of them would lead to public
humiliation at the least and possible beating to death at worst.
Mao modelled himself explicitly on the First Emperor.

Knowing their history, people dug holes in the walls of their
houses and hid their precious treasures – be they family photos,
letters, jewels, statues of the gods or books. The great Tang
Shan earthquake in 1976 killed around half a million people.
One thing which surprised rescuers was how many substantial-
looking and often older houses had collapsed. One reason for
this was that the walls had been so hollowed out to hide family
treasures, they had become weakened.

The books were also hidden in another way. The Book of
Songs and the *Shang Shu* arose from oral tradition – from reciting
the songs and events at ceremonial occasions or in the evenings in
the homes of the great as well as by the fireplaces of the ordinary
people. As with scholars of the Qur'an today, the ability to recite
an entire sacred book would have been considered a sign of great
holiness or worthiness. So some of the texts survived in the minds
and memories of the scholars who outlived the events of the First
Emperor's reign and its immediate aftermath – civil war followed
by the rise of a new dynasty, the Han.

The hero of this part of the story is Fu Sheng. He had been
the Imperial Historian under the First Emperor – a rather dangerous occupation, to put it mildly. Forewarned of the planned
ban on private ownership, he dug a hole in the wall of his house
and hid books including the *Shang Shu*. He then fled into exile.

Decades later, when it was safe to return, he dug the books out of the wall. But tragically only about a quarter of the *Shang Shu* had survived the nearly forty years of its immurement. Just twenty-eight chapters survived, and it was from these that he taught his disciples. The versions he had produced for teaching were written in the revised characters that had been brought in thirty or so years before in order to standardize the use of characters across a united China. For this reason, and very confusingly, this version, the *oldest* version of the *Shang Shu*, is called the New Version or Text. The texts he used probably dated back at least eight hundred years and in one or two cases such as chapter seven, even further. Lying behind many of them there may well be an even earlier oral history, a fact which is perhaps borne out most clearly in the use of sets of four-character sentences within many of the older texts. This could take us back to perhaps as long ago as the mid-second millennium BC.

Around the same time as Fu Sheng's discoveries, a further chapter, which is now in three parts and forms chapters twenty-seven to twenty-nine of the official text, was found – also hidden in a wall – and this was added to those found by Fu Sheng. However, it is possible that this was the first of the forgeries.

Then another version appeared. During the renovation of the home of Confucius in Qufu, another immured text appeared. This one was written in the old style of characters. It was translated into the modern style by Kong Anguo, a descendant of Confucius. This version had fifty-eight chapters, including the twenty-eight that Fu Sheng had found. Because it was originally written in the old-style characters, it is called the Old Text or Version. Because it was a fuller text, it was this version which eventually gained greatest popularity and laid the foundations for what is now the Canonical Version.

However, for a while the New Text was given greater status. For example, when the Emperor Ling Ti of the Han had the Classics carved on stone between AD 175 and 183, it was the New Text which was used. These stone classics were however destroyed very soon after, in the wars which brought down the Han dynasty.

In the mid-third century the Classics were again carved on

stone and this time the pattern was set for the future because it was the Old Text that was chosen. Yet once again these were destroyed in the fall of the Jin dynasty in AD 311. And once again it seemed the *Shang Shu* might disappear.

When the Jin regained control in AD 317, the Court sought versions of the Classics in order to start again. It was at this point that a version was presented by Mei Ze which was called the *Kong Anguo Shang Shu* – named after the original finder and translator of the Old Text.

It is now that doubt enters in. While the New Text chapters are all there and seem to have the ring of authenticity, the other chapters have long been suspected of being reworkings or even downright inventions of Mei Ze. It is these that are seen as fourth-century forgeries.

The final stage in this extraordinary saga is that, early in the Tang dynasty, a final authorized edition was published in 653 and carved on stone stele by imperial order in 837. This set of stone carvings from which all subsequent copies have come – including the one I have used for this translation – still survives to this day. It can be seen in the Forest of Steles Museum in Xi'an, Shaanxi Province, China. It is the *Kong Anguo Shang Shu* presented by Mei Ze in the fourth century AD. Interestingly, it is titled 'Shang Shu', not 'Shu Jing', though the sign in front of it for visitors calls it the 'Book of History – Shu Jing'.

In recent years archaeology has added to our knowledge of what survived. Tombs in Jingmen, Hubei Province dating to the third to second centuries BC have yielded bamboo books including sections of the *Shang Shu*. In some of these, entirely new texts have been found – presumably part of the 100 chapters that we know Confucius wrote about, of which only twenty-eight survived for Fu Sheng to rediscover. Other texts, such as chapter seventeen, We are both Straightforward Virtuous Men, and chapters twenty-one to twenty-three – 'The Mandate of Yue, parts I to III' – are not there in these early texts.

Below is a now established list of what are seen as the earliest texts from Fu Sheng's twenty-eight chapters and what are seen as later texts from Mei Ze's text.

Chapters of the *Shang Shu*

A. Earliest Texts, possibly as old as c. fourteenth century BC to sixth century BC

Chapters:

1	18–20	37	46
2	24	38	47
3	25	39	50
4	26	40	51
5	30	41	55
6	32	42	56
7	34	43	57
10	35	44	58

B. Later Texts – Possibly contain early material but may have been recomposed in the third to fourth centuries AD

Chapters:

3	13	31	49
8	14–16	33	52
9	17	36	53
11	21–23	45	54
12	27–29	48	

Critical Study of the *Shang Shu*

What is truly remarkable about China is that respect for the authenticity of books such as the *Shang Shu* was challenged so very early on. Doubts were being expressed by the sixth century AD, and a full-scale assault on the authenticity of the *Shang Shu* was mounted by scholars in the twelfth century. For example, the great Neo-Confucian scholar Wu Yu in the first half of the twelfth century dismissed large sections of the *Shang*

Shu as forgeries. Critical exploration of ancient and especially sacred texts in the West only really started – for example, with the Bible or Homer – in the early nineteenth century.

The origin of such critical studies lies partially in the desire of these scholars to find the true history of ancient China and in part was also a response to the uncritical way the *Shang Shu* was being studied and applied by conventional Confucians. In particular, these critical studies arose from the Neo-Confucian School associated with Zhu Xi (AD 1130 to 1200), which sought to revive a serious study of the past in order to revitalize the moral energy of the Confucian tradition, not least in response to the growth of other religious and philosophical traditions such as Buddhism and Daoism.

The critical study of the *Shang Shu* was also a major feature of the intellectual debate surrounding the revival of the Five Classics under the foreign invader dynasty of the Qing in the late seventeenth and early eighteenth century AD. The Mongol Qing were keen to appear to be the legitimate heirs of ancient Chinese tradition and quoted the Mandate of Heaven as part of their justification for invading and conquering a corrupt Ming dynasty (1644). To bolster their position, they ordered a reissue of the major Classics and funded this venture magnificently. By doing so they hoped to show that they were more respectful of Chinese tradition and culture than the previous, ethnically Chinese, dynasty.

This provoked fury and outrage amongst some in the Chinese elite and renewed the critical, even dismissive, attitude towards these ancient Classics, building on the work of the twelfth-century Neo-Confucians.

The introduction of Western influences in the second half of the nineteenth century brought a further round of cynicism and scepticism. The Confucian Tradition was seen by radical young Chinese as a block to the modernization of China and as remnants of a discredited imperial past. Even before the 1911 Revolution which overthrew the last dynasty, the old order of Imperial Exams based on the Confucian Classics was thrown out and indeed viewed as obscurantist. They viewed the exams, with their focus on repetition of key sections of the Classics as the root of all problems, as holding back intellectual development in China. Problems which were set in the exams could only really relate to issues explored in the Classics and whilst moral and philosophical topics could be examined in this way, contemporary issues of modernization and the collapse of the older structures of Chinese society under the massive changes of the dying days of the Qing Dynasty were thought to be far beyond the reach of the Classics and their rote-learning by students.

Throughout much of the twentieth century, Confucius and the traditions and texts surrounding his name were simply rejected out of hand or made the target of mass campaigns: for example, the 'Criticize Lin: Criticize Confucius' Campaign launched in 1973, which lasted until the end of the Cultural Revolution in 1976. Lin was the disgraced former Prime Minister of China who reputedly died in a plane crash in Mongolia as he fled to the Soviet Union. His being linked with Confucius emphasized the attack on treacherous advisors.

Only gradually have the Confucian Tradition and its Classics returned to some sort of favour as China has sought to rediscover its roots and to try and see what it means to have a distinct, historical, moral and philosophical culture. Interest in its Classics has revived amongst many who mourn the destruction that hardline Communism and in particular the Cultural Revolution of 1966–76 wrought upon Chinese culture. For the second time in 2,300 years, a ruler sought to destroy all knowledge and understanding of China's past. For the second time in 2,300 years, the *Shang Shu* has come to symbolize the survival of an ancient tradition, a tradition of virtue and of good governance capable of confronting the evils of corrupt, megalomaniac rulers.

In the search for values and virtue in today's China, the words of Minister Yue to the young Shang king in chapter twenty-two ring as true today as they did 3,700 years ago, or whenever they were actually written down in China's past:

Just do what is right and proper and then all will be well.

Martin Palmer
Easter Sunday, 2014

Note on the Translation

In undertaking any translation, the translator is as much an interpreter as a literal translator. In trying to make the images, myths, legends, proverbs and styles of a completely different culture accessible, you have to interpret as much as translate. In this translation I draw attention to this with the very first line of the first chapter, as I have mentioned above. The literal translation would be along the lines of 'It is said that if we investigate back into antiquity'. I have chosen to interpret this as the beginning of a story about the ancient past and its heroes, so have used the phrase 'Long, long ago' as a way of opening a story about the distant past which will be familiar to Western readers. It is perhaps also worth pointing out that ancient Chinese is terse. The first line contains only four characters from which any translator – or indeed native speaker – has to construct meaning.

I have also rearranged the order of paragraphs where the meaning becomes clearer by using a more traditional, Western way of constructing a paragraph. This has meant that at times I have moved a line or two from near the beginning of a paragraph or from the middle and put it towards the end as this enhanced the meaning of the paragraph.

Occasionally, as I did in my translation of *Chuang Tzu* (*Zhuang Zi*), I have not translated every name if that name only appears once and has no particular relevance or role. This applies to some personal names as well as occasionally a place name.

What became clear as we worked on the translation is that there are distinct sections where a rhythm is discernable which indicates either a poem *per se* or a text which through oral tradition has become rounded and balanced by poetic meter in order to aid memorizing. It is interesting to note that the pattern is typical of the Zhou Dynasty style of poetry. This uses the traditional four-word rhythm – a classic example of the imprint of the oral tradition, as this is easy to remember – but broken at the end or at some stage in the poem by the use of an irregular line. In many cases in the *Shang Shu*, this is in the form of a five-word rhythm.*

Therefore I have reflected this in the translation and not treated every sentence as if it had no distinctive pattern, which is what other translations have tended to do. In discerning these patterns of poetry and prose, we have sought to bring to life texts which come from many different centuries, many different hands and which have very many different styles between them, from heroic saga to bureaucratic lists, via official documents of policy. I am grateful to Jay Ramsay's poetic and prose reworking of some of the key sections, which inspired me to see similar patterns in other sections of the book.

In so doing I hope we have been able to breathe life again into a text which through Confucian conformity and the pressures of rote learning had come to be seen as worthy but perhaps rather dull. It is not. It is as diverse and fascinating as any ancient collection of texts – be that the Bible, the Rig Vedas or the Babylonian texts. It is also still an invaluable guide to how to live a virtuous life and how to interpret our place within a moral cosmos. And perhaps it can once again play a role in restraining or removing bad rulers who offend against Heaven and do nothing to help the lives of 'the ordinary people'.

Martin Palmer
Easter Sunday, 2014

---

* See page 273 of Henri Maspero, *China in Antiquity*, translated by Frank A. Kierman Jr, Dawson, Folkestone, Kent, UK edition, 1978.

The Poet and the Text

In a book of such antiquity, it is useful to reflect on how its contents would have been received *as a living word*, learned by heart, and also (as Martin Palmer has indicated) ritually performed on an anniversary basis. The equivalent in our own culture would certainly be closer to drama and liturgy than prose; for example, in the medieval Mystery Plays. For us working on this book, this spoke of poetry in an oral context; and also as a result of our previous work together on the Chinese Classics in the mid-1990s when we found such patterns in the *Tao Te Ching* (*Dao De Jing*), the *I Ching* (*Yi Jing*) and the 100 quatrains of *Kuan Yin*.

Some of this text here is anyway overtly poetry ('The Lament of the Five Sons'); some gaps of lost text may well have been filled with material from the contemporaneous *Book of Songs*, but also, as Martin noted on close inspection, the irregular beat of 4, 4, 4, 4, 5 infuses a whole series of wisdom sayings that are scattered like pearls through the narrative.

And in an early chapter (two), as the Emperor speaks to Kui, we find explicitly this:

> Show them that poetry is the way
> to express their deepest feelings
> shared also through its singing
> where the notes can harmonize
> with the feelings evoked . . .

So to bring this material alive as it deserves for a modern readership, both orally and on the page, we felt that poetry at points

throughout the text was more than justified. It was required. I
was working from Martin's literal translation, finding rhythm
in the lines as blank verse that could also be spoken aloud.
Martin subsequently brought in his own poetic rendition, particularly in the long, explicitly Confucian sequence of chapters
which form the bulk of the Book of Zhou and especially chapters thirty-five to fifty-eight as strategic relief in all the more
lyrical moments he could find within its more prose-orientated
essential statements of morality.

There are two kinds of poetry in our translation here overall.
The first is reflective, philosophical and metaphysical, concern-
ing statements about the Dao (or Way), De (virtue), about
Heaven as the first principle behind everything (and always
above and beyond the ruler or emperor), the Five Elements and
the other elemental building blocks of the Chinese universe.
For example (in chapter sixteen), in wisdom that prefigures the
Dao De Jing:

> Where virtue is, order is there too.
> Where virtue isn't – chaos.
> Follow the design of order and all will go well.
> Ignore it and it will end in disaster.
> A wise ruler is constantly thoughtful in what he follows.

The second involves speeches made by key characters, often in
dialogue, sometimes as dramatic monologue. A striking example
is from the Viscount of Wei in chapter twenty-six:

> Now disaster is poised to come down
> and I must acknowledge my part in this. When we fall,
> I will never serve as a minister again.
> So listen to me, my master.
> Leave, as fast as you can – escape.
> I did not serve you as well as I should have –
> but now, listen to me – and run!
> Otherwise we face complete annihilation.

> We each have to make our own decision,
> and we'll each have to answer for this to our ancestors,
> but I have chosen to stay. My refuge is here.

Here, we found ourselves thinking about Shakespeare in his military plays, where history is re-enacted in the present moment on the stage (Henry V before Agincourt again) in a way that is also timeless. And it is the timeless quality of this material that brings it beyond being just a record of long-forgotten events and into a symbolic realm of truth – as with the *Yi Jing*. These rulers and their supporting courtly cast of officials represent what can and needs to be if ruling a country is going to succeed 'under Heaven'. We should also never forget what happens when that mandate is withdrawn and a kind of egotistical hell takes its place – as true for Zhou as it was 2,500 years later with the despotic and wife-executing Henry VIII. Sadly, or perhaps inevitably, this is as relevant today as it ever was, with the presence of self-elected dictators who are by definition incapable of recognizing anything beyond their own drive for power and who always (by definition) damage their own people. Their demise may be as inevitable as the Shang dynasty, but it is equally important to wonder where the spiritual world leaders of today are, and how can they come into being without a recognition of the Higher Self that Heaven symbolizes that is informing and guiding them?

And of course we may think about what that means for all of us, and what it means to stay with Heaven in our own actions with all their consequences, on the eternal (and karmic) path of self-realization.

Jay Ramsay

SHANG SHU
SHU JING

THE BOOK OF YU

According to the traditional chronology of China, Emperor Yao ruled between 2355 and 2285 BC. The flood referred to here and throughout the early chapters was the Great Flood of Chinese mythology set around 2300 BC and against which various heroes struggled.

THE CHRONICLE OF YAO

Long, long ago there lived the Emperor Yao. He was known to everyone in the land as truly noble. He was attentive, bright, cultured, graceful and he was all these things without effort. He was also sincere, able and his reputation lit up the four corners of the world, reaching from Heaven itself down to Earth. In him were combined all that was best from his ancestors and all that will be best of the generations to come. As a result, he was enlightened and virtuous and so he was able to make sure that the whole world lived in balance and harmony. This meant everyone lived in a state of enlightenment and even the surrounding states and tribes lived peacefully.

To make sure that the people would know the passage of the seasons in their proper order, he commanded two officials, Xi and He, to study and compile information concerning the vastness of Heaven and the movements of the sun, moon and stars so that the calendar could be properly organized. From this he commanded one of the younger brothers to go to the Yang Valley of the Sunrise and reverently observe the rising of the sun in the east. This was so he could determine when the spring equinox would take place and by observing the stars he could know when the day and night were of equal length. This meant the people would know when it was time to return to work in the fields and they could see this was also when the birds and animals started to mate.

On top of this, he commanded another brother to go south and to stay there to note the summer solstice and its stars, which would tell the people when the day is the longest and they could then know to hurry up with their labours. This is also the time when the birds and animal start to moult.

Another brother was commanded to go to the west to the place known as the Yin Valley and there to note the autumn equinox. Observing the stars, he could then calculate when the days were of equal length. This meant the people could know it was the season for resting and that the birds and animals were at their healthiest.

Finally he commanded his fourth brother to go north to the place known as the Dismal City to study the winter and the stars in order to know when the winter solstice falls. This is a time when the people stay warm indoors, while the birds and animals have their winter coats and hibernate.

From all this the Emperor was then able to say: 'Let me explain that the year has three hundred and sixty-six days and by adding an additional month we can balance the seasons. Knowing this, we can appoint the appropriate officials and all will be well.'

Then the Emperor added: 'But can anyone find me a man who can understand all the four seasons, who can work with me and be the judge of what is good?'

'What about your heir, the Crown Prince? He seems very bright,' one of his ministers answered.

'Sadly, thinking he will be the heir, he has become a trouble-maker, so that proposal is not realistic,' the Emperor replied. 'What I need is a wise minister. Can anyone find one for me?'

'Well, there is the Minister of Labour, who seems pretty competent,' another minister answered.

In reply the Emperor said: 'Sadly he says one thing in public and another thing in private. In public he seems to be very respectful and humble but his vanity rises like a flood to the very Gates of Heaven. Oh, by all that is holy, the ceaseless floods and the vast waters are destroying everything that is good and right. The dark waters have overwhelmed the hills and moun-tains. They have raged right up to Heaven itself while the people below, why, they are in despair. Is there anyone who can help?'

All his ministers replied, 'Well what about Gun?'

To which the Emperor retorted, 'Good grief, no! That man is a rebel who goes against whatever is right and refuses to be disciplined.'

'But why not at least give him a try?' implored the ministers.

So it was that the Emperor said to Gun, 'Go and see what you can do.'

For nine years Gun struggled, trying to succeed at the task set him, but he failed.

The Emperor said, 'Oh, by all that is holy, I have now been Emperor for seventy years. Can't someone take up the Mandate of Heaven from me so I can resign?'

'But there is no one with sufficient virtue, no one worthy enough to sit on the throne,' replied his distraught ministers.

So the Emperor commanded: 'Seek out the most worthy; go and look amongst the humblest of the people.'

The ministers said: 'Well, we have heard of one such humble person called Yu Shun,' to which the Emperor replied: 'Good idea! I have heard of him. What is he like?'

'His father is a blind musician who is a fool and his stepmother is without principle. While his brother – he is a total prig! However, being a pious and loyal son, he has managed to create such harmony within the home that all of them have become better people as a result,' the ministers replied.

The Emperor said: 'I will test him out by marrying him to my two daughters.'

So saying, he commanded that his two daughters* be sent to Yu Shun and that they should marry him. And the Emperor commanded them: 'Do what is right.'

* Polygamy or having a concubine as well as an official wife was normative until very recently in China.

Yu is the title given to Shun when he became Emperor in around 2285 BC.

2

THE CHRONICLE OF SHUN

Long, long ago there lived the Emperor Shun. He was known as a person of great solemnity. Like the Emperor Yao who ruled before him, he was renowned for his wisdom, his culture, his intellect, his integrity and his virtue. It was clear from all these qualities that he had the Mandate of Heaven.

He was passionate about ensuring harmony and balance,
through observing the five virtues of loyalty.
He personally attended to the smooth running
of every part of the bureaucracy on an annual basis.
He entertained leaders
from every corner of the Empire
with great solemnity
and once,
even though he was caught in a terrifying storm,
he nevertheless never gave up on his intention
to visit and see for himself the
vast flooded lands of the foothills.

Shun ascended to the throne because the old Emperor Yao had tested him and had said, 'Come, my dear Shun. For three years I have tested you, listened to you and seen that you do what you say. Now ascend the Imperial Throne.' Even so, Shun initially felt unworthy of such a position – so you can see how virtuous he was.

It was on New Year's Day that he was finally made Emperor,

in a ritual in the Temple of the Ancestors. Here, using the glorious celestial instruments, he observed the Seven Heavenly Bodies* which influence events on earth. Through rituals he offered his respect to the Heavenly Emperor as well as to the six key elements of the cosmos, and he worshipped all the deities of nature through the medium of the mountains and the rivers. Having himself received the Five Tablets of Authority, he brought together at the auspicious time all those whom he appointed to govern the Empire and bestowed upon them their own Tablets of Authority.

It was in the second month that he began his official journeys of investigation by going east. He started at Mount Tai, where he offered sacrifices. And then he offered sacrifices in turn to all the auspicious mountains and rivers symbolizing the whole country. The rulers of the East came and offered homage. This made it possible for him to enforce the laws and make sure all the proper procedures were followed and get the calendar sorted out and agreed. He standardized the rituals associated with the tones of music and the proper weights for the chimes. He made sure the officials knew what was expected of them. Indeed, he regulated everything, from the number of colours to the correct numbers of sacrificial animals – two alive to one dead, for example. Only when he saw everything was going well did he confirm the key officials in their posts.

It was the fifth month when he went south on his official journey of investigation, conducting the proper sacrifices at the Southern Sacred Mountain [Southern Mount Heng] just as he had done at Mount Tai.

By the eighth month he was in the West on his official journey of investigation, travelling as far as the Western Sacred Mountain [Mount Hua], where once again he offered the proper sacrifices.

Finally, in the eleventh month, his official journeys of investigation took him to the Northern Sacred Mountain [Northern

---

* Thought to be the sun, moon and five planets known to ancient Chinese astronomy.

Mount Heng] and here he carried out the same ritual sacrifices as he had done in the West.

When he celebrated his return home, he offered a sacrifice to the Noble Ancestor.

It became his tradition that every five years he would set off on three of these official journeys of investigation. This involved the nobles and princes each reporting to him on the state of affairs in their own regions and it required them to come before him personally. Once he had studied these reports in detail and was satisfied, he rewarded the nobles and princes with appropriate gifts such as chariots and invested them with splendid robes. He created twelve regions and appointed to each a sacred mountain while also dredging the rivers to help them flow through their channels.

He took special interest and care in defining punishments. He ordered that mutilation or execution should be replaced by banishment, that offending officials should be whipped, that scholars who were unworthy should be caned and that fines should be brought in as compensation for crimes. If someone did something wrong by mistake or ignorance, they were to be pardoned, but anyone who abused their power, and did so constantly, was to suffer the most extreme punishment – execution. His watchwords were 'Beware! Beware!' and he attempted to moderate punishment with compassion.

There were four notorious villains and he dealt with them all. He exiled one to an island, sending another to a more remote island, despatching one chieftain and his whole tribe [Miao people] to a remote mountain fastness while one villain was kept as a prisoner until the day he died. And as a result, everyone was pleased.

After twenty-eight years, the old Emperor Yao died, his souls ascending and descending,* and his people mourned him as they would their parents. For three years all music was banned throughout the land.

---

* In traditional Chinese belief, a person has two souls. One, known as *bo*, is seen as yin and therefore earthly, to which it returns at death. The other soul is known as *hun* and is seen as yang – heavenly, which is where it ascends.

On New Year's Day, Shun processed to the Temple of the Ancestors. He consulted with the four guardians and discussed how to throw open the doors so that he could see and hear everything. In his quest for understanding he consulted the twelve judges and gave this advice: 'Our supply of food depends upon the seasons; be thoughtful to those far away; take care of those close at hand; respect the virtuous; trust the generous; disregard the false. This is how the mob will be helped to accept your rule.'

'Alas', said Shun, 'you four great ones, can you name anyone who is so worthy that they can undertake the Emperor's plans? Anyone who I could name as the Prime Minister? Anyone who can help me to sort things out?'

'There is the Lord Yu,' said everybody. 'He has been in charge of the Great Works [against the flood].'

'Well now, Yu,' said the Emperor, when Yu arrived. 'You have triumphed over the waters of the flood and created dry land. Go and get on with all this.'

Yu bowed low but recommended that there were three others, Lords Qi, Xie and Gaoyao, who were better suited to this role. However, the Emperor replied: 'That is all very well but it is you I have chosen to get on with this.'

Next the Emperor said to Qi: 'Qi, the people are suffering for lack of food. I want you to go and run the Ministry of Agriculture and ensure the proper sowing of seeds.'

The Emperor turned to Xie and said: 'The people are rebellious and the proper order of society is ignored. It will be your special role to be the Minister of Education and to teach them, and indeed encourage them, to observe the proper order of society according to our traditions. Engage with the people and encourage them to be kind.'

Turning to Gaoyao, the Emperor said: 'The barbarians are attacking our lands, robbing, murdering, plundering and creating mayhem. I want you to become the Minister for Justice. Use the full force of punishments; restrain them according to the full force of the law and making public examples of them for major offences, or exile them to remote areas for lesser offences. Do this wisely and this will mean you are obeyed.'

Next the Emperor asked, 'Who can oversee the major Works and their workers?'

'Chu,' replied everyone.

The Emperor turned to Chui and said, 'Having discussed this, I have decided to appoint you as Minister of Works.'

Chui bowed low but did not want to accept. Instead he recommended three other people, but the Emperor said, 'Well, now! You see I have chosen you as I believe you can take charge.'

Turning to the Court, the Emperor said, 'Who is there that really knows this country from top to bottom? Who will care for the land from the plains to the forests; who will care for all nature?'

The court replied, 'Yi – that's the one.'

Turning to Yi, the Emperor said, 'I have decided to appoint you especially to take charge of my lands.' Yi bowed low but declined, saying that there were four others who were much better suited to this task.

'Well, that's as may be,' said the Emperor, 'but it is you that I want to do this.'

The Emperor one day said, 'So, my four great ones, is there anyone capable of undertaking the great rituals honouring Heaven, Earth and the deities?'

To which everyone replied, 'My Lord Yi.'

So the Emperor called the Lord Yi to him and said, 'You must be in charge of the Temple of the Ancestors. Day and night you must oversee that the offerings are made with due reverence. Be pure and honest.'

The Lord Yi bowed low but recommended that Kui or Long were much better suited. However, the Emperor replied, 'I want you to do this. Do as you are told.'

Then he turned to Kui and said:

'Destiny has chosen you
to facilitate the music
and train the young.

Teach them to be honest but also mindful
to be generous but also circumspect

to be strong but also receptive
to be firm – but not arrogant!

Show them that poetry is the way
to express their deepest feelings
shared also through its singing
where the notes can harmonize
with the feelings evoked
  – just as the reed notates the voice –
and the eight instruments effect a harmony.

With this, harmony and balance
are brought both to the people
and the deities.'

Kui said, 'Of course. I will sound the finely tuned chime stone and all creation will be moved by this.'

Turning to Long, the Emperor said, 'I hate slanderous talk and evil behaviour. This disturbs the people. So you will be my Minister of Information and you will communicate night and day for me and brief me on the reality of what is happening.'

'So,' said the Emperor to all those whom he had appointed, 'do as commanded and undertake in conjunction with Heaven itself these responsibilities. Every three years I will test you and after three such examinations, the weak ones will be dismissed while the brightest ones will be promoted.' As a result of this, all the officials undertook their duties properly and the Miao people were exiled.

Rising to power at the age of thirty, for thirty years he was in power and for fifty years he was the Emperor. Then he died, his souls ascending and descending.

Yu the Great was the hero who defeated the Great Flood and is one of the most revered of ancient Chinese figures. As Emperor, he is traditionally the founder of the Xia Dynasty (2205 to 1766 BC).

3

THE COUNSELS OF
YU THE GREAT

Long, long ago there lived the hero Yu the Great, known for his virtuous way of life. He was admired for this throughout the land, and in response he declared: 'If a ruler knows how to rule properly and if this is echoed in the conduct of the officials and the execution of their responsibilities, then the Affairs of State will run smoothly. This will encourage the people to be both keen and honest.'

'The fact is,' added the Emperor Shun, 'good ideas will never be lost. No one who is worthy and hard-working will be neglected and as a result everywhere in our vast country will be at peace. However. Pay attention to everything; put aside your own desires in order that you can serve others; do not oppress the poor and unfortunate. The Emperor is the one who ensures this happens.'

Yu replied to him:

'It is your virtue which makes this possible. It is your combination of wisdom, devotion, resoluteness and culture, which shows that Heaven has given you its Mandate. As a result you have authority over the Empire and everything under Heaven comes within your sphere of leadership.

'Doing what is right brings its own blessings,' Yu added. 'If

you follow what is evil, disaster comes. It is the difference
between the shadow and the echo.'*
The Emperor responded:

'But be on your guard! Especially
when there doesn't seem any reason to be so.
Never be deaf to the teachings of the law
or waste your time on fruitless high living.
Don't indulge yourself stupidly, or be loose
and if you have good people in place
don't let others come between you.
Renouncing evil, don't be distracted
by insubstantial and ego-driven plans.
Do *what is right by your own light*
never do what isn't just to win praise.
Don't oppose the people's will, either
just because you can. The result?
Even those rough barbarians who surround us
will agree to be ruled by you!'

'This is so, oh Emperor,' said Yu.
'And bear in mind that true virtue is the basis of good governance, and governance is deemed to be good if it contributes to the
well-being of the people. See how the cosmos regulates the Five
Elements of water, fire, metal, wood and earth in order that it
functions properly. Therefore, uphold virtue and this will increase
well-being; support creativity and this will help balance all life.
And if everything goes well, celebrate! Have a festival! Guide the
people wisely by using fear of the law; create odes and sagas and
sing of these achievements so that they are never forgotten.'
The Emperor responded:
'When Heaven is in control and Earth obedient, then all creation will be in balance; all things will be in harmony. This will
be the monument to your achievements.'

* The shadow is seen as more real because it comes directly from the physical
body whereas the echo can fool you as it is often hard if not impossible to tell
from where it really originates. Thus the shadow is seen as the virtuous path
while the echo is not.

'Now pay attention dear Yu,' said the Emperor. 'I have been emperor for thirty-three years and age and time have affected me. In guiding the people, watch out for laziness in particular.'

Yu replied:

'I am not worthy of the people's trust. However, Gaoyao is a very virtuous man. Everything he does is worthy, which is why the people trust and respect him. My Emperor, why don't you consider him? For myself, I always think of him. Even if I try to think of someone else, I always come back to him. If I hear his name mentioned, then I think, "Oh yes, he's the one." He is constantly in my thoughts. I urge you, my Emperor, to consider him and his merit.'

Then, turning to Gaoyao, the Emperor said:

'Because you are the High Judge, I know that no one, neither my ministers nor my people, will break the law. Using the power of punishment, you have taught the people of all ages to honour and respect the True Law and so everyone is governed well. Because you used restraints, the people no longer need to be made to follow the Middle Path: they just will do so naturally. Just keep on like this.'

Gaoyao replied:

'Most revered emperor, you're truly admirable.
You consult but never condescend
you guide everyone generously. With you
wrongdoing doesn't descend to succeeding generations –
only the best that's been accomplished.

If failure was because of a genuine error
you pardon it however great
but however small a deliberate transgression
you penalize it.

Where there's doubt about a case, you're forgiving
where there's uncertainty about the clarity
you always err on the side of benevolence.

Instead of just killing someone who may be innocent

you will choose discretion, not the letter of the law
and because you love virtue that is life-affirming
this has touched the hearts of everyone
so that they no longer need to be controlled.'

The Emperor responded:

'You are like the wind that breathes across the land
touching everyone, so that what I want my government to
do you've already done by your example.'

Then, turning to Yu, the Emperor said:

'When the Great Flood threatened to overwhelm us
you did as you promised and showed us
just how dependable and capable you are!
It is clear you are uniquely suited to govern.
You were unending in your labours
for the country's benefit, barely giving a thought
to your own family, your own home.

And you managed this without puffing out your chest
and so it was you proved yourself
uniquely qualified to govern, free of all pride.
There's no one else under Heaven to compare with you
– no one can even try.

I can say in all honesty that no one under Heaven
can claim to be more honourable than you!

It's clear that Heaven means you to govern
and that you'll rise to the prime role of responsibility.

The heart and mind of the people is fickle.
So be careful: be constant, stay on the Middle Path.

Don't be seduced by false promises
or follow badly thought-out plans.

A leader should be loved. Who should be feared? *The
  people*.

If a country has no leader
then who can inspire respect?

And what about a leader who has no people?
Who will defend the country then?

Regard your position of authority
with respect and exquisite care.

Progress what is needed. And remember:
Heaven's blessing will cease for ever
if there's despair and poverty in your lands.

Remember: from the mouth comes both what is good
and what leads to wars. I won't say it again.'

Yu said, 'Let me seek advice through divination regarding
which are the worthy ministers, and follow its advice.'

The Emperor replied, 'Yu. The Diviner makes his decision
first, then he consults the Great Tortoise Shell in order to determine if this is the Will of Heaven. Likewise I make up my mind
and only then do I consult with everyone. They then agree that
this is what fate decrees and even the deities concur – indeed all
the forms of divination agree. When divination gives such a full
answer, you don't do it again.'

Yu bowed low, but he resolutely refused to accept.

'Do not refuse,' commanded the Emperor. 'It has to be you.'

So it was that on New Year's Day Yu embraced his fate
(the Mandate of Heaven) in the Temple of the Ancestors and
became chief amongst the ministers, as the Emperor himself
had insisted.

The Emperor said to Yu, 'Sadly, the leader of the Miao
people refuses to acknowledge me and submit. It is time for this
to end.'

Yu ordered the princes to assemble with their troops and he addressed the army.

'Listen to me, my legions. The Miao Leader is stupid. He is foolish, arrogant and rude! He is vicious and violent, but even as he turns away from the proper path he pretends he is a man of honour. He brings destruction through the rebellion he leads. Virtuous men are driven away and petty men are promoted in their place. The people have turned against him and will not come to his defence. Heaven rains down disasters upon him. I have summoned this mighty host in order to punish him. Let us march forth, united in our strength, of one mind to triumph!'

The fight against the Miao went on for a very long time, until Lord Yi came to Yu's assistance.

He said: 'Only virtue can inspire Heaven to come and nothing can prevent it. Pride goes before a fall while humility brings greatness. This is the Way (Dao) of Heaven.'*

The Emperor had been at Mount Lei and he went out into the fields every day and wept. He called upon Compassionate Heaven and upon his parents and took full responsibility and blamed himself. He attended to his duties and showed such respect to the captive leader of the Miao, and looked after him so well, that the leader was reformed. This sort of sincerity is capable of moving the deities themselves – so it is not surprising that it touched the leader of the Miao.

Yu honoured these wise decisions and said:

'Indeed this is so.'

And so saying, he led his army away. The Emperor set the example of virtue and wisdom to the whole country. In celebration they performed the dance of the shields and feathers between the two staircases in the Great Court of the Emperor and within seventy days the Miao had surrendered.

* The term here refers to the Way (Dao) as a moral path in comparison to the later Daoist understanding of the Way (Dao) as a spiritual truth about the nature of existence.

Gaoyao is considered a model of the just Confucian-style official.

4

THE COUNSELS OF GAOYAO

It is said that back in the mists of time, Gaoyao, the Minister of Justice, said: 'Harmony will be honoured if people can clearly see that virtue is maintained.'

To this Prime Minister Yu replied, 'True. But why?'

'Well now,' said Gaoyao:

'Someone who's aware of their own development
will be gracious and mindful of whoever he deals with
regardless of rank or title. This will touch others, too
who are intelligent enough to grasp it, and be of service.

By facing up to what's in front of him, he also secures the
future.'

Yu was moved by these luminous words, and said, 'This is so true.'

Gaoyao responded:

'It is, really, and it comes about
through understanding the way people react
and by making them feel safe and secure.'

'Sadly, even for the great Emperor Yao this was hard to achieve,' Yu said. 'If you can understand the needs and desires of the people, then you can give them appropriate roles and duties. When the people feel secure, this moves the ruler, and his people are inclined to view him with affection. A leader who is this wise need not fear troubles with foreigners on his borders. Why be worried about lies, duplicity and conspiracies?'

Pondering upon this, Gaoyao said: 'In reality there are the nine virtues and if someone has these, then such a person, in our experience, will always act appropriately.'

'And what are these?' asked Yu.

Gaoyao replied, 'They are, in sequence:

generosity balanced by discipline
evenness balanced by resolve
willingness balanced by respect
confidence balanced by reverence
assurance balanced by boldness
directness balanced by gentleness
simplicity balanced by discernment
verve balanced by integrity
courage balanced by justice.

'Anyone with this kind of integrity will always be successful. If three of these virtues shape how you behave day by day, then this will bring enlightenment to everyone in the family. If you conduct yourself day by day with six of these virtues, then the beloved homeland will be well governed. If all nine virtues are the basis of your life, then all will be well for everyone. This is how those few people in charge of the many will ensure that everything is done in balance with the foundational elements of the universe itself.

'To restrain extravagance and indolence in the country, make sure the leaders don't indulge in such behaviour themselves. Quite seriously, be very careful of this. A myriad of problems can arise within the space of even one or two days, so don't appoint worthless officials. Heaven mandates what will happen and we are just its agents.

'Heaven has decreed the five duties of obligation and hierarchy for us, with their concomitant responsibilities. Heaven has mandated the five levels of the universe and these give rise to our five rites, which we have to conduct accordingly. If these are properly observed, then all life is united and in harmony.

'Likewise, Heaven has decreed the appropriate rewards to specific virtues and these we signify through the five different sets of official robes. Heaven has also decreed how punishments will be measured, and we must follow this pattern, for this is how government should be enacted. So let's get going!

'Heaven, like us, sees clearly and hears clearly. Heaven inspires awe and rewards accordingly and this the people can see clearly. Heaven and Earth, above and below, everything is linked. And as a result, wise men will take their responsibilities within this order very seriously.'

Finally Gaoyao said, 'What I say is true and this is how things are.'

Yu replied, 'Indeed, and when what you say is translated into action, all goes well.'

Gaoyao said modestly, 'I am not that wise, but by grace, every day I hope to be of assistance, and as a result the government will perform well.'

5
YI AND QI

'Now Yu,' said the Emperor Shun. 'You have a lot to tell me, I think.'

Prime Minister Yu bowed to the Emperor and said, 'My dear Emperor, what can I say? As you know, I have always tried to work hard every day.'

To this Gaoyao responded, 'This has been a sad burden for you. How have you managed it?'

Yu replied:

'The Great Flood came from Heaven itself and threatened the very mountains and hills. The people were overwhelmed and very frightened. Travelling by whatever means I could, I traversed the hills, cutting down trees for defence with Yi, and teaching the people to make themselves stronger by eating meat. I drained the waters into nine channels and sent the waters towards the sea. I had drainage ditches and canals cleared so they could flow into the rivers.

'Together with Lord Qi I taught the people how to grow crops to supplement their diet of meat. I encouraged trade and ensured the proper management of surplus so that everyone would have enough to eat. In these ways I ensured the country was once again well governed and was able to recover.'

'Excellent – this is indeed so,' Gaoyao exclaimed.

'Dear Emperor,' said Yu. 'I tell you truthfully, you must always ensure that you are careful in how you rule.'

'This is indeed true,' said the Emperor.

Reflecting, Yu advised him:

'Be at peace with yourself. Just be yourself and this will ensure unity. Surround yourself with good and wise people and

then all will be well. This will show everyone that your actions
are in accordance with Heaven and that you are blessed because
of the Mandate of Heaven bestowed upon you.'

'Ah, statesmen – they must be ministers and followers; ministers and followers,' said the Emperor.

'Indeed,' Yu replied.

As he reflected, the Emperor said:

'Statesmen: you are my legs, my arms, my ears and eyes.
You can help me to help my people!
I want to be effective in every corner of my land, and I
    need your help.
I need to be aligned to the emblems of the past
which our ancient ones studied and described . . .
the sun, moon, the stars, the mountains
dragons, flowers, and insects
embroidered on the robes. All these symbols:
monkeys, fire, fine rice, the axe
all designed in the finest silk of the five colours.

I want to hear the six notes, and the five tones
played on the eight ritual instruments
and see how these regulate the world. I want to hear
odes and sagas uttered by the universal five
so that you can hear them too. And if
I do wrong, show me what is right
but don't malign me: we must honour everyone in office.

As for those who don't honour the pattern of the seasons
and are out of harmony with the cosmos through
    wrongdoing
once we see their true nature, their punishment
will be to be recorded in the Book of Deeds.
Do our people want people like this?

And what of the masters of Divine Rhythm?
Do they really know how to compose and what to chant?
If they do know, fine. If not, fear will eclipse them.'

Yu said:

'Well, Your Majesty. Your fame has spread everywhere under Heaven, from shore to shore, bringing life to every place and to all people. They are all united in wishing to be Your Majesty's ministers. As a result, you, Your Majesty, will soon be able to promote them. Read their reports and those that shine forth, reward them with chariots and official robes as they deserve. Then everyone will offer loyal service and respect. But, oh my Emperor, if you do not do this in time, then day by day you will hear reports of moral decline.

'Beware of being like Zhidan and his arrogance and extravagant behaviour. He was like that day in, day out. He forced boats to go where there was not enough water. He kept bad company. As a result he lost the throne for not just himself but for his descendants. This I offer as a warning. Remember, even though I had only been married for three days, I left to battle with the flood. Even when my son was born and in distress, I did not return home, so intent was I on solving the problem of controlling the waters. I designed and organized the five key areas – stretching over five thousand *li*.* I appointed twelve officials and within the boundaries of the Four Seas, I appointed five leaders. They all did as I commanded. Only the troublesome Miao refused to do as he was told. Consider this, my Emperor!'

The Emperor said:

'That any virtue exists is due to your example and influence upon others. Gaoyao, for example, follows you and whenever necessary and with a clear conscience punishes anyone who fails to follow.'

Kui said:

'Let us strike the chimes; play the stringed instruments; sing and chant in order to bring the ancestors to visit us. Let us call up the spirit of Yu and all the great leaders of the past.'

With flutes and drums, with rattles and all sorts of other musical instruments, the birds and animals started to dance. At the nine notes, even phoenixes, both male and female, came to dance their stately dances.

---

* A *li* is a Chinese mile, equivalent to roughly half a kilometre.

Kui noted, 'See how, when the ritual music is played, all of life joins in joyfully and all the leaders of the people are happy.'

In celebration, the Emperor composed a song.

'Humanity,
beware of failing to fulfil
Heaven's Mandate.
Be vigilant.'

The Emperor then sang:

'If the ministers are prepared,
the head can act,
and all rulers
will be successful.'

Gaoyao bowed low and said in a commanding voice:

'Listen now.
Hear and take note of what is said.
Your leader will guide you.
Follow his rules.
Pay due respect.
Make sure your behaviour is appropriate.'

Then he sang this song:

'If the head is wise
and the ministers in accord
all will be well.'

He also sang:

'If the head is a pain
and the ministers are lazy
then all will go awry.'

The Emperor greeted everyone and said, 'This is true. Therefore go and do this properly.'

THE BOOK OF XIA

The Xia dynasty traditionally ruled between 2205 and 1766 BC. The first ruler was Yu the Great. The Report to Heaven is one of the most important documents regarding the places, names and administration of Early China.

6

YU'S REPORT TO HEAVEN*

Yu set out and mapped the whole of his land and marked the territories. He noted all the details, from the high mountains and the rivers to the hills.

The detailed report is as follows:

Jizhou Area: initial focus – Hukou

Attention paid to Liang and Qi mountains.
Watercourse near Taiyuan restored.
Waters controlled south at Mount Yue.
In the north, focus on controlling the force of the Zhang river.
Soil: white clay – good.
Tax: highest of the top level.
Fields: average.
Note – Heng and Wei rivers are now cleared and flowing
    smoothly to the sea.
Dalu area now able to be cultivated.
Tribute: from the island-dwelling barbarians – fur.
Route: going to the right of Mount Jieshi, then up the
    Yellow River.

* We have translated this as a Report to Heaven based upon the use in the title of the character for 'Above'.

Yanzhou Area: between the Ji and Yellow River

Nine rivers returned to their proper way.
Leixia is an area of lake once again and functioning properly. Yong
    and Ju rivers flow into it. Mulberry bushes grow here now –
    people have settled here from the hills to cultivate the fields.
Soil: rich and dark. Grass – good; woodlands healthy.
Tax: middling.
Fields: upper middling.
Note – over the past thirteen years productivity has risen.
Tribute: dyes, silks – in special coloured containers.
Route: via the Ji and Ta rivers into the Yellow River.

Qingzhou Area: from Mount Tai to the sea

Waters around Yuyi have been controlled and the Wei and Zi
    rivers returned to their proper way.
Soil: white – along the coast, salty.
Fields: upper lower.
Tax: middle of top level on top quality.
Tribute: salt; matting; wide range of marine products; silks; hemp;
    lead; pine and rare jewels. From the tribe of the Laiyu comes
    silk in baskets.
Route: along the Wei and Ji rivers.

Xuzhou Area: between the seas,
Mount Tai and the Huai River

Huai and Yi rivers controlled; land around the Meng and Yu
    mountains now arable. Flood waters drain on to the plain and
    into a lake – ensuring more cultivable land.
Soil: red clay and abundant flora.
Fields: upper middle.
Tax: middle of top level.
Tribute: five colours earth; bright feathers from the Yu area;
    special wood from Yi mountain; ritual chime stones from the Si
    river; pearls and fish from the Huai valley.
Route: via Huai and Si rivers to the Yellow River.

Yangzhou Area: from Huai River in the north to the southern sea

Flood waters now channelled into the Pengli lake. Islands of the south now habitable as a consequence. The three main rivers have been channelled to flow into the sea. Swamp land drained and now bamboo, grass and trees are abundant.

Soil: muddy.

Fields: poor.

Tax: middle.

Tribute: gold, silver and copper; gems; bamboo; ivory; skins; feathers; fur and timber. From the island people – matting; silk in baskets; varieties of organs.

Route: via Changjiang river to Huai and Si rivers or alternatively along the coast via the above rivers.

Jingzhou Area: from Jing mountains to the south of Heng mountain

Changjiang and Han rivers now controlled and flow like tribute-bearers into the sea. The many tributaries of the Changjiang have been channelled, resulting in prosperous land now around Yunmeng.

Soil: muddy.

Fields: upper middle level.

Tax: upper level.

Tribute: feathers; ox-tails; ivory; rhino hides; gold, silver and copper; various specialist woods; grindstones; flint arrowheads; cinnabar; bamboo and the rare Hu wood. These three areas also send a famous tribute of baskets of pandan, richly coloured silk, pearls and mother-of-pearl, while from the rivers come the giant tortoises.

Route: via Changjiang river and its outlets and the Han River, then by land to the Luo and the Yellow River.

Yuzhou Area: Jing mountain to the Yellow River

The rivers Yi, Chan and Jian now flow into Luo and on into the
  Yellow River. Yingbo lake along with Hoze and Mengzhu lakes
  all help regulate the waters.
Soil: Clay with loam in lower regions.
Fields: Middling.
Tax: Middle upper level.
Tribute: paint; hemp; good to poor quality matting; baskets of
  coloured silk; floss; ritual chime stones.
Route: Luo river into the Yellow River.

Liangzhou Area: South of Hua mountain
to the Black River in the east

Arable land now on Min and Bozhong mountains due to the Tuo
  and Qian rivers being controlled. Cai and Meng mountains
  now cultivatable. The wild people of Heshui valley now
  working the land.
Soil: black.
Fields: upper middle.
Tax: highest.
Tribute: gems; iron; silver; steel; flint arrowheads; chime stones;
  bear, fox and other skins.
Route: from Xiqing mountains along the Heng, Qian and Mian
  Rivers into the Wei River and then into the Yellow River.

Yongzhou Area: between the Black and West Rivers

The Ruo River has been channelled west. The Jing and Wei Rivers
  are united to the north. Channels have been dug to link the Qi
  and Ju Rivers to the Wei from the north and the Feng River
  from the south. The Jing, Qi, Zhongnan, Chongwu and
  Niaoshu mountains were honoured and surveyed. By controlling the rivers and surveying the land around the mountains,
  scope was created for greater agricultural use. The Sanwei area
  was also made habitable and the Miao people settled there.
Soil: yellow.

Fields: the best possible.

Tax: lower middle level.

Tribute: precious jewels such as jade and pearl-like gems; fur and
    leather clothing from the barbaric tribes, Kunlun, Xizhi and
    Qusou.

Route: by land through the Jishi mountains, by boat along the
    Yellow River to the west of Longmen, gathering at the junction
    of the Wei.

Yu also undertook and achieved the following:

Studying and regulating the Qian and Qi mountains.

Travelling on inspection to the Jing mountain.

Crossing the Yellow River, Hukuo and Leishou to Mount
Taiyue.

He went via the Wangun mountains to Dizhu and Xicheng,
then via Taihang and Heng to Jieshi and thus arrived at the sea.

Yu studied and regulated all the rivers from the Xiqing,
Zhuyu and Niaoshu to the Taihua mountains, and then to the
Xiong'er, Waifang, Tongbai and Peiwui mountains.

He studied and regulated the channels along the Bozhong
and Jing mountains and the Neifang and Dabie mountains;

He then channelled the rivers to the south of Min and Heng
mountains via the Jiujiang River to Boyang lake;

He studied and regulated the Ruo River through the Heli
channelling them into the area where the nine rivers flow and
flood;

He studied and regulated the Black River to Sanwei and its
waters now flow into the seas to the south.

He studied and regulated the Yellow River from the Jishi
mountain to Longmen and on south, passing north of Hua
mountain, then via the Dizhu mountain east to Mengjin. From
there he went across the Luo to Dapei. Here he turned north to
the area of the nine rivers where the flood waters of the Yellow
River are poured into the sea.

From Bozhong mountain he studied and regulated the Yang
River, which east of there becomes the Han and then even further east becomes the Canglang. Passing the Three Dykes, it
reaches Dabei, where it turns south and into the Changjiang

River. Going even further east, the surging waters pour into the Pengli lake; then out, heading east as the Beijiang River, it flows into the sea as the Changjiang River.

From the Min mountain, he studied and regulated the Changjiang River, which branching off eastwards becomes the Tuo. Further east the waters flow into the Li River, reaching the area of the nine rivers where it floods, where it flows east and bends north before wandering into the Huai River. From there it flows to the middle Changjiang River and then into the sea.

He studied and regulated the Yan River, calling it the Ji River, which flows east into the Yellow River with its flood plain known as the Ying marshland. Going on east and to the north of Taoqui to the marsh of Ho, it then turns north-east to join the Wen and from there, north, then east, it flows into the sea.

Yu studied and regulated the Huai River from the Tongbo mountains, ensuring it joins the Si and Yi Rivers and from there flows eastwards to the sea.

He studied and regulated the Wei River from the Niaoshu hill to flow into the Feng and then on to the Jing in the east. Further east the Wei passes the Qi and Ju Rivers and then flows into the Yellow River.

Yu studied and regulated the Luo River from Xiong'er, where it flows north-east to join the Jian and Chan Rivers. Here it turns east and flows into the Yi before entering the Yellow River in the north-east.

As a result of Yu's great labour, the waters were regulated throughout the land, making it possible for people to settle. The hills were cleared of scrub and established. The rivers were channelled and the marshes embanked to prevent flooding. It was now possible to reach the capital from anywhere in the land. Material wealth and production increased. The status of the land for taxation purposes was standardized and the exact level judged accordingly. The fields were properly classified with regard to the main types of soil and the tax was fixed.

He bestowed lands and titles, including surnames. Because virtue became the ruling discipline, no one dared to deviate from it.

The inner zone stretched five hundred *li* in each direction from the capital. Within the first one hundred *li*, the income was the entire plant of the grain; from the second, the ears; from the third, the straw; from the fourth, the husks; and from the fifth, the threshed grain.

The land beyond the five hundred *li* was the land of the Nobles. The income from the first hundred *li* in this zone were various types of labour; from the second, specific labour; from the third, military service.

Beyond the land of the Nobles was encompassed the zone of security. In the first three hundred *li* the locals were educated; in the outer two hundred *li* the people were under military rule.

The five hundred *li* area beyond this was the Forbidden Lands, where the first three hundred *li* were for non-Han people and the outer two hundred for convicted criminals.

The five hundred *li* beyond that were the barbaric lands where in the first three hundred *li* the barbarians lived and the two hundred *li* beyond that were where the worst criminals were sent.

From utmost east to the sea; from utmost west to the desert; from utmost north and from utmost south, his fame and power reached everyone. Yu was rewarded with the highest badge of honour – the jade plaque – and his task was over.

This speech is believed to have been given by Yu's son Qi and relates to a rebellion against him around 2193 BC.

7

THE COVENANT AT GAN

The six commanders launched a terrible war at Gan. The king said, 'Well, my six commanders of the army, I have a covenant to make with you. The ruler of Hu has insulted the integrity of the Five Elements and has insolently disregarded the three rituals duties of the year. Heaven has ordained his destruction and having removed the Mandate of Heaven to rule, I am commanded to punish him.

'You, the archers to the left in the chariot, if you do not do your duty, you will have sealed your fate. You, spearmen to the right of the chariot, if you do not do your duty, you will have sealed your fate. Charioteers, if you do not drive your horses forward and engage the enemy, you will have sealed your fate. Do as you are expected and you will be honoured in front of the ancestors. Fail to do as you are expected and you will be executed in front of the gods of the land and your entire family will be enslaved. Or killed.'

The overthrow of Tai Gang took place around 2159 BC.

8

LAMENT OF THE FIVE SONS

Tai Gang sat on the throne like a corpse. He was selfish and thoughtless and totally without virtue, which caused the black-haired people to consider rebelling. This did not distract him at all. He continued to indulge himself even more and went off to hunt by the River Lo. He was gone for a hundred days without any indication of when he would bother to come back.

Because of this, and seeing the people could not stand this any more, King Yi, the ruler of Jiong, opposed Tai Gang and forced him to the Yellow River. The five brothers of the emperor accompanied their mother dutifully, and went with her to await their brother beside the River Lo. The five sons all spoke out and reiterated the ancient warning of Yu the Great. They did this through singing songs.

The first sang:

> *Our inspired ancestor proclaimed*
> *that the people should be cherished*
> *and never abused!*
> *The people are a country's foundation;*
> *if the base is secure, so is the country.*
> *When I look out at the world*
> *and see the ordinary people, men and women,*
> *any one of them could be better than me.*
> *I am just one man –*
> *always capable of getting it wrong.*
> *Should I really wait until their anger blazes?*
> *Better to anticipate it before it emerges.*

In front of the great crowd of the people
I should be braced as if I were driving a team of horses
with reins that are rotting!
The man who rules over everyone
needs to be conscious of what he does.

The second son then sang:

It's all there in the teachings:
If, at home, you lead an outrageous life
and abroad go lusting for the chase
wasting yourself in heavy boozing
dancing and carousing the night away
in your buildings with their carved ceilings
and sumptuous suggestive walls
it has to be said that these
will always lead to your downfall!

The third son followed:

Once there was Tang of Tao
a model man of the path
who was the ruler of Ji.
But we wasted his exemplary way
now the laws and rules are in chaos
and everything is in pieces!

The fourth son replied:

Our ancestor was luminously bright,
emperor of states beyond measure.
He had rules, he had order
he handed down to his descendants.
He regulated weights and measures
so precious that he stored them in his palace!
All of this vanished through thoughtlessness,
leaving our ancestors' sacrifices stranded.

The fifth son sang alone then:

I am desolate,
where can I hide
to contemplate these terrible thoughts?
The mass of the people are against us!
Who can we trust?
My heart is weary.
This lack of virtue makes me so ashamed.
My face reddens.
I try to think, but how can they ever be forgiven?

9

THE PUNISHMENT OF YIN

When Zhong Kang became king, the Prince of Yin was ordered to take charge of the army hosts. The officials Xi and He had neglected their duties because they got drunk the whole time in their home towns and as a result the king ordered the Prince of Yin to punish them.

'Well now, my brave warriors,' the Prince told his assembled warriors. 'Our wise one of the past has spoken clearly to us, and so he has kept our land safe. Our illustrious forebears respected Heaven's decrees and were also wary of them. The ministers in those times did as they were expected and they were constant in the execution of their duties. The officials also did what was expected. Thus was the ruler able to be clear and thoughtful in all his actions.

'Every year, in the first days of spring, someone travels abroad, banging a wooden board and announcing that officials should get ready and that workers should prepare their tools for the tasks ahead. If they weren't ready and prepared, then there was an appropriate punishment awaiting.

'At this very moment the officials Xi and He are sunk deep in a drunken state. They have abandoned every vestige of virtue, have abused their office and have abandoned their responsibilities. As a result they have disturbed the Order of Heaven and this is down to their ignoring their duties.

'For example, on the first day of the third month of autumn, there was a solar eclipse in the constellation of Fang. The blind musicians beat their drums to drive away evil forces while the petty officials rode off in great haste and the people panicked.

Through all of this Xi and He sat like corpses, hearing nothing and understanding nothing. They were totally at a loss to explain what Heaven was doing and as a result they have been charged with the death penalty – which has been the conse-quence of this kind of behaviour from the earliest times. The regulations clearly state that if the eclipse comes after their pre-diction, then they must be executed. Likewise if the eclipse comes before their prediction, they must also be put to death. And there can be no exception in either case.

'As a consequence, my army and I have Heaven's authority to punish them. So, my warriors, let's be united on behalf of our Royal Regime. Together, you and I will carry out the Man-date of Heaven's Son. When a raging fire roars from the volcano of Mount Gun, it throws out jewels as well as burning stones, side by side. Likewise, when Heaven's decrees are executed with passion and dedication, the consequences are even more ferocious. Therefore, I will destroy the chief culprits, though I will leave their followers alone. Those who have become cor-rupted will be reformed. Well, indeed, when order is above compassion, then things can be sorted out. But if compassion is above order, then no good will come of any of it.

'Now my warriors, forward. But take care.'

THE BOOK OF SHANG

Tang is the first ruler of the Shang dynasty – later also called Yin, after their new capital. They traditionally ruled from 1766 to 1122 BC. He is later referred to as Tang the Conqueror, as he overthrew the corrupt Xia and set the first model of the Mandate of Heaven moving from one dynasty to another through revolt.

THE COVENANT OF TANG

King Tang said, 'Gather to me all my people and listen carefully to what I have to say. It is not me, ordinary little me, who has the audacity to rise up here. But it is Heaven that has decreed that the ruler of Xia must be executed, because of all his many crimes.

'Now, you warriors, you are telling me, "Our leader has no thought for us and our needs. He summons us from our work and he does this just to punish Xia." I hear what you say, but the ruler of Xia has sinned and because I am in awe of the Supreme Ruler, I have no option but to undertake this task.

'But I hear you asking, "Of what significance is Xia to us?" Well, the King of Xia has brutally oppressed his people and drained their energy. And the people, why, they have lost all hope and they are crying out, begging, "Is it not time for the sun to die so that we can die also?" So you can see that the ruler of Xia's lack of virtue leaves me with no option but to go ahead and do this.

'If you, my people, will join me, a simple solitary man, in carrying out Heaven's decree, then great will be your reward. Do not doubt me, my people. I will not go back on my words. So, if you do not honour my oath and do as I say, my people, I will kill you and all your children. And I will show no mercy whatsoever.'

THE SOLEMN PLEDGE
OF ZHONGHUI

When Tang the Conqueror banished Jei to the south, being a virtuous man he was troubled by this deed and said, 'I am afraid that future generations will speak ill of me because of this.'

'Come now,' replied Zhonghui. 'Heaven gives each generation the passions which can lead to disaster if they're not guided. However, Heaven also gives each generation a number of people who are wise. And in time, they will come to control these passions and impulses. Let's be frank, the ruler of Xia lost sight of what is virtuous. As a result, the people were living in a state of great fear. This is why Heaven gave our king the courage and the wisdom so he can show the many states of our land how to behave well. He can be guided by the ancient ways of Yu the Great, and therefore he can be worthy of the Mandate of Heaven.

'The King of Xia caused offence by his false claims that he has the blessing of the Supreme Heaven and that, as a result, he has the right to decide what the people should and shouldn't do. This is not how an emperor should behave and this is why the Shang have been given the Mandate of Heaven – because of our love of justice, and so that we can become the teachers of all the people.

'In order to try and seem to be more in control, the Xia not only ignored the wise people but also ridiculed them – while busily promoting and praising the powerful. This is why we Shang were at first of no significance to the ruler of Xia. We were like weeds in a field of ripe corn. Our people, great or small, lived in constant fear of persecution, even though they hadn't done anything wrong. Our leader, being a virtuous man, could not help but speak out against it and you can imagine how this led to his actions being publicly criticized by others.

'So our king did not go near wild, licentious parties. Nor was he interested in personal wealth or prosperity. Instead, he gave offices to people who were really virtuous, appropriate to their integrity. And he gave great rewards to people who strove to do good deeds. He knew that if he treated others as he would treat himself; if he corrected himself, as he would correct others who do wrong; if he was truly just and benevolent . . . Why, then the people would trust him.

'Do you remember how the ruler of Ge attacked those innocent people who were generously bringing materials for the sacrifice? And Tang had to take matters into his own hands? Yet when he restored order in the east, the barbarians in the west complained. When he did the same in the south, those in the north complained, asking, "Why does he ignore us?" No matter where he went, people rejoiced, saying, "We have longed for so long for our prince to come and now that he has, all is well again." This is why the people's support and admiration for the Shang is so well established.

> 'In other words,
> judge who is capable and work with the virtuous;
> pick out who's loyal and encourage the good;
> support the weak and square up to the stubborn;
> challenge the rebels and chasten the dissolute.
> If you do this, whatever is failing will simply collapse
> while whatever is good will flourish –
> that's how a country can be run successfully.

'After all, a virtuous ruler who lives like this every day is admired, while a selfish and wilful ruler ends up losing everyone's affection.

'Let this be seen in you, my King, and the people will be able to perceive such marvellous virtue, the Middle Way of living. Act justly. Think and feel in your heart what is right and then you will set an example for the future.

'As the old saying goes, "He who knows that he needs to learn from the wise will be successful. He who thinks that no one is his equal will fail. He who asks will be rewarded. He who relies on himself will lose."

'For goodness' sake! If you want a good ending, ensure a sound beginning. Promote the careful and reject the wastrels and you will be following the Way of Heaven. And as a result, you will be awarded the Mandate of Heaven.'

12

THE DECLARATION
OF TANG

When King Tang came home after the conquest of the Xia, he came to Bo and there – before all the people – he made this declaration.

'My people,' said the king. 'All of you, from every region of the land, listen carefully to what I (a straightforward man) am about to say. The Emperor above all Emperors has endowed every person with a moral sense, and this is their essential, original nature. However, to ensure that they stay true to this essential nature, it is necessary to have rulers.

'The King of Xia lost sight of virtue and became an oppressive dictator. He even oppressed you, my dear people from every region. And when you were no longer able to bear his bitter and poisonous ways, wrought through his cruel regime, you united to proclaim your innocence before everything in Heaven and everything on Earth. You know it is the Way of Heaven to bring good fortune to the good and to curse the wicked. This is why Heaven has brought disaster upon the Xia, making their terrible sins apparent to everyone.

'This is why I, unimportant as I am, like a child
have been granted the Mandate of Heaven
which lights up the whole world with its authority.
I cannot ignore it or stop doing what is asked of me.
To prove this, I will now offer this dark-skinned sacrifice
to highlight the Supreme Heavenly Sovereign Spirit
and the depths of the crimes of the Xia!

I have asked the Supreme Heavenly Sovereign Spirit to
      join me
combining our strengths, and to request from Heaven
its authority to be granted to all of you men
so that together we can vanquish the oppressor! Be assured.

The Mandate of Heaven cannot fail.

You, my people, are like the buds and the flowers –
you have come forth. This is my cause, my reason.
I must resolve this for once and for all
simple man that I am, so that all will be well
for you – and also your families.

And I worry that I might disturb anything in the cosmos,
this makes me tremble with anticipation
as if I was standing on the edge of a precipice . . .

In the new world I am creating
rebellion and conspiracy will not be necessary.
If everyone follows the laws as given
then Heaven will bless us in what we do. It is simple.
If you do what is right, I will know it too.
And if I make mistakes, I won't try to exonerate them
but instead search deeply within myself to make sure
that all is done according to the heart and mind of Heaven.

If anyone anywhere does something wrong
then the responsibility will lie with me
 – I say this again as a straight-talking man!
And if I do something wrong, you may also be assured
that no blame will fall on you.

Come now, let us all strive to be true to this
and everything will go well!'

Yi Yin is respected alongside Gaoyao as a model of the Confucian-style official.

13

THE TEACHINGS OF YI

It was in the first year, in the twelfth month and on the second day of that month that Yi made sacrifices to the Ancestor Kings and also presented the heir apparent to them. All the princes were there and the officials arrived in order to receive their duties and responsibilities from the king's minister.

'Come now,' Yi said, addressing them all. 'In the past the Xia started off by being worthy, so as a result no wrath descended upon them from Heaven. The spirits of the land and waters were at peace and all life on earth was united – all creatures. However, their descendants did not follow this model, and as a result the Emperor of Heaven sent disasters upon them, through our ruler whom Heaven chose to endow with its Mandate. The uprising started at Ming Tiao and our attack at Bo. Truly, our King of Shang displayed the holiness of his power by freeing the people from oppression and the people celebrated this generous action with joy.

'Now then, arising from such reward for virtue, everything hangs on how you all begin. Start by showing true affection to your own family because if you can show it to them, then you can go on to show it to the State and then to everyone within the boundaries of our land.

'Come now. Our Ancestor Kings reflected on what it is that

holds people together. They listened carefully, and they never ignored what they were told but instead followed the advice they were offered. If they were in the highest position, they showed vision; if in a lowly position, they showed loyalty. They took people at face value and reserved criticism for their own faults – and as a result they ruled over all the lands. How incredible was that!

'They gathered around them people who could contribute, not just to their well-being but also to the well-being of all of you, the heirs of all this. They set out the codes of punishment and warned the officials, saying, "If you dare to waste your time holding parties in your homes and drinking yourselves senseless, imagining this gives you magical powers, or if you spend your time thinking only of making a fortune and dreaming of women or if you dissipate yourselves by wandering around or hunting, then you will know yourselves for the disgraces that you are. If you insult the wise, oppose the loyal and true disregard your elders and virtuous people and instead mix with adolescents – then everyone will see you're in disarray. These sorts of worthless attitudes and evil practices can so easily destroy your whole family. If a ruler did that, his kingdom would be ruined. Any official who fails to prevent such actions will be punished by being branded with irons."

'Go and teach this to all the young, and to the scholars.'

King Tai Jia came to the throne following the death of Tang and the previous chapter refers to this new king. Yi Yin is the same person as Yi in the previous chapter.

14

INSTRUCTIONS TO KING TAI JIA, PART I

When the new king ascended to the throne, he did not follow the ways of the Counsellor and as a result Chief Minister Yi Yin wrote to him.

'The First King paid close attention to the clear Mandate of Heaven,' he wrote. 'And as a result he was in perfect harmony with everything in the cosmos. He was in harmony with the spirits and demons, with the gods of the land and of the harvest, with the ancestors and the shrines, all of which he venerated. Heaven studied his every virtue and gave him its Mandate so he could bring peace and submission to all the many regions of this land. Later, Yin was able to assist the ruler in bringing order to the people and this is why you, as the next heir, have inherited such law and order.

'Now I myself, Prince Yin, have seen in the western region of Xia that when it was governed well, all went well for its ministers. However, when it was then governed without reference to good governance, its ministers suffered. So, let your heirs be very careful and note this. Because if they do not, then they will only bring dishonour upon their Ancestor.'

The young king rejected this advice with a few dismissive words.

Yi Yin wrote to him again, saying, 'The First King, long before every dawn broke in the sky, would sit quietly waiting for the sunrise, contemplating and seeking understanding. He filled his court with people who were competent and virtuous so they would guide and instruct him. Do not be so foolish as to ignore this, because if you do it will cause your downfall. Be patient and plan properly for the future. Think how the archer makes sure his arrow is pointing in the right direction before he fires. Choose your target and then follow the model set by your ancestors. Not only will I be pleased but all generations will praise you in the future.'

The young king was seriously not interested.

Yi Yin then said to him, 'This is frankly not good enough. Your attitude has become a bad habit of yours and I can't just leave you here amongst the dissolute.'

So he built a palace for the young king at Tong, close to the tomb and shrine of the First King, where he could reflect upon his life so far and reform himself.

The new king went to the palace and he was distressed by his former behaviour, repenting and bemoaning, until at long last he was able to be truly virtuous.

15

THE INSTRUCTIONS TO
KING TAI JIA, PART II

In the third year of his reign, on the first day of the twelfth month, Yi Yin escorted the young king to Bo, where he was formally robed and crowned.

Yi Yin wrote down the following words:

> A people without a ruler
> can't live a productive life
> because there is no order.

> A ruler without a people
> can't govern a country.

> You, my king, have been chosen
> by the Emperor of Heaven himself
> who bestowed on the Shang
> the ability to be virtuous
> – a blessing that will last
> for ten thousand generations.

The king covered his face with his hands and kowtowed, saying, 'I was like a child, unable to see clearly how to be virtuous. I was dissolute, I ignored all that was right and proper. I violated all the precedents and frankly I was rushing headlong into ruin. While it is possible to handle disasters from Heaven, there is no escape from the disasters we bring upon ourselves. My dear teacher, I know that I have spurned your advice in the past. That was how it all began. Now, I wish to benefit from your advice so the future can be so much better.'

Yi Yin covered his face with his hands and kowtowed and said, 'If you can really be sincere and virtuous and can follow the will of your ancestors, then you will be a good ruler. The First King cared like a child for the poor and for those who suffered, and as a result the people were happy to obey him – indeed, they did so cheerfully. For example, when he was visiting one area, the people in the neighbouring areas would say they couldn't wait for him to visit them, because whenever he visited, injustice would cease.

'Dear King, be virtuous. Model yourself on your worthy ancestor. Do not indulge in negligence but instead, when you reflect upon your ancestors, consider the importance of filial piety. When you give orders to those under you, do so gracefully. When planning for the future, make sure you have clarity of vision. When contemplating virtue, listen carefully. Then I will be able to serve Your Majesty without ceasing.'

16

INSTRUCTIONS TO
KING TAI JIA, PART III

Yi Yin once again spoke sincerely to the king.

'Come now, my king. As you know, Heaven does not have favourites. It simply rewards those who are respectful. It is the same with the people. They are not uncritical in their affection because they look to see who is really benevolent. The gods don't just accept any offering made to them. They only accept those offered with real sincerity. As you know, it's not easy to sit on the throne Heaven bestows.

'Where virtue is, order is there too.
Where virtue isn't – chaos.
Follow the design of order and all will go well.
Ignore it and it will end in disaster.
A wise ruler is constantly thoughtful in what he follows.

'The First King was diligent in cultivating virtue and as a result was worthy to be the agent of the Supreme Emperor. Now that you're king, focus your attention on this model.

'Remember that to rise,
you have to start at the bottom.
To travel a long way
you have to start with your first step.
Never look down on ordinary people;
they always have their load to bear.
Never be complacent on your throne;
there is always danger.

'Start as you mean to continue: so when someone advises you to do something that goes against your own instinct, examine it to see if he is right. When someone agrees with you, examine it to see if they are in fact mistaken.

'This is how it is.
Without trying, nothing worthwhile can be achieved.
Without awareness, nothing can be achieved either!
If a straightforward man is honourable
then everything will be in harmony throughout the land.
But if a ruler ignores these words of wisdom
then there will be confusion.

A true minister doesn't hang on to his position, either,
once the work is done.

Follow this counsel, and your country will be content.'

17

WE ARE BOTH STRAIGHTFORWARD VIRTUOUS MEN

When Yi Yin had managed to restore the rule of law, he told the king he wanted to retire. However, first of all he set out his understanding of virtue, saying:

'Heaven is really hard to understand. Its Mandate with a ruler is not a constant one. If the ruler is virtuous and constant, then he will retain his throne. If he is not constant and virtuous, then he will lose everything. The King of Xia was not constant in his virtue. He ignored the spirits and oppressed the people and as a consequence the Heavenly Emperor no longer cared for him. Instead a search was made throughout the land for one upon whom Heaven's Mandate could be bestowed. Someone who was straightforward and virtuous, and who could rule over all the spirits. Both Tang the Conqueror and I, Prince Yin, are straightforward in our virtue and so, when we touched the heart and mind of Heaven, the love of Heaven rewarded us with a clear mandate and we took charge of everything. As a consequence, we had the power to remove the Xia from their control of the world.

'Do not for a moment think Heaven was especially inclined to favour the Shang. Its favour was given because we are both straightforward virtuous men. Nor was it the case that the Shang sought the support of the ordinary people. It's simple – the people respect straightforward virtue because when virtue is straightforward it always brings good fortune. However, if virtue is without focus and all over the place, it is inevitable that it will spell disaster. Good or evil, happiness or disaster – none of these comes without there being a cause, and Heaven decides which it is to be based upon virtue.

'Now then, my young king, you are new to this Mandate so you must ensure you have renewed your virtue. From first to last, have this as your only goal, so it simply becomes part of what you do every single day. When you are choosing officials and ministers, make sure they are thoughtful and considerate men. Those who serve those above them must work to ensure that the virtue of those above them is upheld, because this will in turn cause those below them to ensure their well-being in turn. This is not easy, so special attention is required to ensure both harmony and simplicity. There is no supreme rule for virtue – it is simply judged by how good it is. Nor is there anything inevitable about what is good – it simply comes from simplicity. Everyone knows this and therefore they say, "How wonderful are the words of our king. What a heart and mind he has. Because of this we know that he is a worthy heir to the First King because he cares for the lives of all his people."

'Well, now. If you were to go back seven generations and find that every generation had been virtuous, that would indeed be worthy of praise. Furthermore, to be celebrated as the head of the ten thousand families is a sign of the appreciation of the good order you have created.

'After all, a ruler without people is not a ruler, while a people without a ruler cannot serve. Never show off in order to intimidate others. If your people are unable to live virtuously, then clearly their ruler has been unable to do what is right.'

King Pan Geng reigned traditionally from 1401 to 1374 BC and it was under him that the capital was moved to a new site, Yin, hence the change of name for the dynasty.

18

KING PAN GENG, PART I

Pan Geng had decided to move the capital to Yin, but none of his people wanted to go there with him.

So he sent out a herald to all the most quarrelsome people he could find and he said, 'Our king chose this place to settle because he cared for the people who otherwise would have died. But now, in this place, we are no longer able to help each other, which is why I asked the diviners for a divination. The reply has come and it says that this new place is a good place to settle. Remember how in the past, whenever there was an important decision to be made, the First King respectfully followed the commands of Heaven. What he took care to avoid was following his own inclinations and nor did he decide to rather stay in just one place. This can be seen by the fact that the capital has moved five times.

'Now, if we do not follow this example from ancient times, who knows, maybe Heaven will revoke its Mandate to us because we can't even follow such a clear example from the First King. Let's be like a tree that has been cut down and yet from its stump come vigorous new shoots. In the same way, Heaven will continue to place its trust with us for a new life in this new place. As a result, the glory of the First King's era will return and peace will come to the land once more.'

In deciding to teach the people, King Pan Geng started with the officials, by reminding them of what was expected of them.

'Do not let any of you ignore the poor people,' he said. 'It is the will of the king that everyone should be welcome here.'

What the king then went on to say basically was that: 'Every one of you – every one of the vast multitude – is welcome and I myself will be your guide. Forget all the pettiness and stop being lazy. In the ancient past our First King only offered positions of authority to those from aristocratic families. The king made the decisions and no one tried to hide them. As a result, the king trusted them and so there was no need for any double-dealing. This in turn led to a transformation amongst the people.

But now, you are all kicking up a great fuss, making false and pointless claims, and I honestly have no idea what you are all going on about. It is not that I have given up on virtue, but you don't give me any respect. It's as if you cannot see me for who I really am, a straightforward man – as if you are looking at me by the faint light of an open fire. I fear that, through my lack of experience, I am to blame for this. After all, a fishing net only works if all the many strands are in place and holding together. Likewise, a farmer who puts time and trouble into managing his fields will get a good harvest as a result. If you can banish selfishness, then you will help the people and indeed your own family and friends as well. If so, then you could claim to be virtuous. Instead, I fear you're like a lazy farmer who never bothers with hard work, so has a poor harvest – and you seem not to be troubled by problems from afar or even close at hand. Instead of speaking kindly to the heads of the families, you gossip and act immorally, which only brings disaster upon you. What an example of evil you officials have become to the people, and now you will reap the consequences, even as you try to reform.

'And what about the poor? They try to tell you what is wrong but you only tell them lies in reply. To me you act so very differently because you know I can decide whether your life will be long or short. Why don't you tell me the truth instead of stirring things up with your falsehoods, alarming the people and causing nothing but distress? Don't you know that once a fire has been started in the fields it cannot be put out? I am not going to take responsibility for all this.

'Chi Ren has said, "In the case of men we want those from old families. In the case of music we want new instruments."

'In the ancient past our First King shared both the delights and labours of ruling with your predecessors and forebears. This is why I cannot act unjustly. Their efforts have been noted down the centuries and so I cannot fail to honour your efforts. When I offer the sacrifices to the First King, your ancestors alongside him are honoured as well. They bring both blessings and disasters – but I cannot reward virtue when it is not there.

'Let everyone do what they can and do their utmost to fulfil these plans, if you will listen to me, a straightforward man. With me, what you see is what there is.

'Those who are criminals will die. Those who are good will be honoured for their virtue. The country will only prosper if you all contribute. So any failure will lie with me, the straight-forward man, and that will be because I have neglected to punish. I am telling you all this so that from now on you will focus on your duties. You must do what is expected of you and stop slandering each other.

'Because if you don't, you will be punished. And then it will be too late to repent.'

19

KING PAN GENG, PART II

Pan Geng rose up and with his people crossed the River He, having decided to relocate them. To encourage them to follow him, he decided to speak to them, hoping that they would agree to go with him. They came, having been warned not to cause trouble in the Royal Palace. Addressing them, he said, 'Pay attention to what I say because I am going to be as clear as possible. Do not fail to listen to what I have decided.

'Indeed,' the king said. 'Long ago there was mutual respect and deep affection between my ancestors and the people, because my ancestors cared deeply for the people. This meant that when troubles came upon them from Heaven, they were able to survive. However, when such troubles came, our kings did not just sit around trying to work out what to do. They were worried about the people, so they took firm action. So how come you have all forgotten this?

'I have commanded you to move because I want everything to go well for you all. I am not punishing you for some offence. I have commanded you to move to the new capital simply because I am concerned with your well-being and because this will help you live more fully. This move will also help to stabilize the State. But you, you don't seem to care about the things that afflict my heart and mind. Nor have you told me of what you are worried about, because if such concerns were sincere and honourable they might well influence me – because I am after all a straightforward man. The result of all this is that you end up worried and stressed.

'Think of this situation like a boat. Unless you're careful about when you sail, you could end up losing the whole cargo.

Currently we are not in agreement and therefore could end up drifting into disaster. What is even worse is that you won't honestly face this, and you have become so agitated that I cannot see how you ever will! Because you don't plan for the future – or, to be honest, even for what is about to happen – you simply build up your levels of anxiety and egg each other on to greater levels of stress. You just live for the present with no thought for the future. Living like this, you cannot just hope that help will come in the nick of time from above.

'It is my intention that you should come to a common mind about this, putting aside evil thoughts that afflict you in both body and mind. I believe that by obeying the Mandate that comes from Heaven, life will be better. Am I acting like a dictator, exerting my influence over you? I only do this because it will be good for you in the long run. Reflecting upon how my illustrious ancestors cared for your ancestors, I feel a responsibility to act in a similar way towards you.

'If instead of governing in such a manner I was instead to hang around here, then the High Ruler would pour disasters and woes down on my head, asking, "Why are you oppressing the people?" If you, the mass of the people, do not seek to live life fully, and trust me with one heart and mind in this action, me, a straightforward man, then our First Ancestors will pour disasters upon you. They will say, "Why do you not do as your ancestors wish, but instead act without virtue?" When punishment comes from above upon you, you will not be able to escape.

'Long ago, my Noble Ancestors worked to take care of your ancestors and fathers. This is what I am trying to do, but you insist on thinking badly of me. My Noble Ancestors cared for your ancestors and fathers, and if you are not careful, your ancestors and fathers will reject you now and won't even attempt to save you from sudden death.

'Now I have here my ministers who share responsibility with me. But they don't care for anything except their own fortunes. I can tell you that their ancestors and fathers are appalled and have complained to the High Ruler, saying, "Punish these, our descendants, severely." The High Ruler is left in no doubt that such a punishment should be sent down upon them.

'Indeed, you need to understand clearly that I will not be diverted from my plans. Do not be so foolish as to stand in the way of this Great Plan. Instead, let us all now be united. Agree to be part of my plans and then you will find that your hearts and minds can be faithful to me. However, if anyone continues to be stubborn or to rebel, disregarding my orders without fear – indeed using every opportunity to plan treason – then I will cut off their noses. I will utterly destroy them. I will wipe out their lineage and none will be allowed into the new city.

'So, instead: go! Carry on living properly and I will transfer you to the new place and your families will live there for ever more.'

20

KING PAN GENG, PART III

Pan Geng successfully completed the move.

He gave the people their places to live and the roles they were to fulfil and then spoke to reassure them.

'Do not be petty minded or lazy, but instead work hard and ensure that you create a great destiny in this place. I have shown you how every part of me – from my heart to my very entrails – longs for this. So now you know my plans. I will no longer treat anyone as if they were a criminal, just so long as you put aside all anger and do not create groups in opposition to me. For I am a straightforward man.

'Long, long ago my noble ancestor the King wanted to be even more virtuous than his forebears. He moved the people to The Hill, away from the danger of the Floods and likewise away from the evils and dangers surrounding the people. As a result of this virtuous act, he brought prosperity to all the people.

'Once again my people are vulnerable and the floods have left you with no safe place to live. So let me ask you this. Why do you think you are being uprooted, all my people, and moved? The Supreme Ruler wishes to restore again the virtue of our High Ancestor and bring once again prosperity to our House.

'Obeying the Mandate we have received, my advisors and I have chosen this place as our new, everlasting settlement. Because I am just a young man, I obviously did not want to go against such a plan, but I also sought good advice through divination. This is why this plan is now even greater.

'Indeed, my princes and officials, I wish you could share this vision and enthusiasm with me. I watch over you and seek to guide you, wanting nothing but the best for my people. Therefore I will not appoint people who think it is clever to be greedy. No, I will appoint those who will care deeply for the well-being of all and whose actions are shaped by compassion for all, and that way I'll make sure this settlement succeeds.

'So, you know where I stand on all this. Don't fail me. Don't seek wealth and treasures. Instead, look for the well-being of the people. By showing your virtue, you will ensure we are all of one heart and one mind.'

We skip over two reigns to come to Wu Ding, who reigned from 1324 to 1264 BC. Yue here is later referred to as Fu.

21

THE MANDATE OF YUE, PART I

The king rightly mourned for the prescribed period of three years. However, when this time had passed, he still did not speak. His statesmen were very worried by this and remonstrated with him.

'Indeed,' they said. 'A wise man is said to be illustrious and an illustrious man is an inspiration for others. The Son of Heaven of course rules alone over the vast territories and the ranks of officials who all respect his authority. However, the will of the king is only known if he speaks. If he says nothing, the statesmen have no idea what to do next.'

In response, the king wrote the following:

'I do not speak because although I am the ruler of the Four Quarters I do not feel virtuous enough to tackle the tasks ahead. I must tell you that while I was in a state of grace, meditating on the proper way ahead, I had a dream sent from on high. I saw that I had been bestowed a good advisor who would speak for me.'

The king then described the person he had seen in his dream and had a portrait made of him, which was sent throughout the land. As a result, it was found that only a man called Yue, then living in the wilderness of Fu Yan, fitted the description.

As a result, the king appointed him as his Prime Minister and as his constant advisor.

He commanded him:

'Every morning, every evening
tell me what you think so I can act virtuously.

If I'm like hard metal
then you will be my grindstone
on which I find my edge.

If I'm like one trying to cross a great river
then you will be my boat I'm rowing across.

If I am like a dry and thirsty land
then you will be rain to me!

Being honest you will make me so.
Be like a medicine, which, bitter as it is
is healing for the patient.

I am a man walking barefoot,
I need to tread carefully or my feet will be hurt.

'Along with my officials I want you to help me be vigilant
and of one mind with you. This way I can be worthy of my
Ancestor Kings and follow myself the One who bestows from
on High in order that everyone will be at peace. Indeed, respect
my will at this time for the unity of all our desires.'

Yue replied to the king:

'Just as a carpenter is able to make a piece of wood straight,
so a ruler who has the wisdom of a sage will himself become a
sage. As a result, the statesmen will know what to do without
waiting to be told. So it is that no one would dream of refusing
to do with reverence what the king desires.'

22

THE MANDATE OF YUE, PART II

Once Yue had taken up the mandate to be in charge of all the officials, he went to see the king.

'Indeed,' he said. 'A wise king follows the Way of Heaven when founding his state, when setting up his capital city, as he appoints his liege princes, nobles and great officers – as well as all the others he needs to appoint. He doesn't just do what he wants but what will be good for the people.

'Only Heaven is all-wise, but a sage will ensure that his style is based upon Heaven and this in turn will be the model of inspiration for his statesmen. As a result, the people will be properly governed. Remember, words can cause disgrace and weapons cause wars. Formal robes should be worn with due reason and ceremony and the sword should only be used after careful consideration. Your Majesty should be careful and therefore wise and then all will be clear.

'Both good and bad government depend upon the calibre of the officials. Never give such positions to those who are simply favourites, but because they are actually reliable. Likewise, never give praise to those who are wicked, but only to the virtuous.

'Think very carefully about how you want to influence people, and when the time is right, influence them positively.

'When you think you are good, that's the moment when goodness departs! Or if you think you are skilful, then skill vanishes too.

'Be fully prepared, then as a result things won't go wrong.

'If you show favouritism, then you will be seen with contempt.

Don't think too highly of yourself – serious mistakes are the consequence!

'Just do what is right and proper and all will be well.

'Lack of awareness and carelessness in ritual practice leads to a general lack of reverence. When ceremonies are just seen as a burden, this seeds contempt and confusion. Serving the deities becomes really difficult as a result.'

The King replied, 'Yue, this is excellent. Your words inspire us to do what is right. Without your advice I would not have known what to do.'

Yue kowtowed and said, 'It is not that hard to understand but it is difficult to do what is right. As Your Majesty now understands this, all should be well and you will be ranked alongside your Ancestor Kings in virtue. If I, Yue, had not spoken like this, I should have been the one to blame.'

23
THE MANDATE OF YUE, PART III

The king said:

'Come closer, Yue.
Insignificant as I am
I studied under Gan Pan:
then I lived an austere life.

I went to the River He
and from there to the Bo.

As a result, you know
I'm not that well-versed in worldly things.

Will you sit with me now
and guide me about the right things to do?

I want you to be to me
like fermentation is to wine
or like salt and prunes are in a fine soup!

Help me to improve, don't walk on by.
Let me do my best to follow your advice.'

'My king,' Yue replied. 'Folk strive to understand things in order to make their plans work. To be honest, the ancient teachings should be enough to ensure such success.

'To want to be successful so your family can rule for ever but without paying any attention to the wisdom of the past ...

Well, frankly this is something I have never heard before. In study there needs to be humility and the wish to persist and from this comes an increase in understanding. Reflect upon such wisdom and virtue will arise within. For a model, look at your Ancestor Kings and you will not fail. If you do this, then I, Yue, can respect you and as a result it will be possible to find worthy people to appoint to the key posts.'

'Indeed,' the king responded to Yue. 'If everyone in my kingdom comes to respect my virtue, this will be due to you. A good statesman needs a sage in the same way that a human being needs arms and legs. I recollect that in the past a former Prime Minister said, "If I fail to bring the mind of my Prince to be in line with that of Yao and Shun, then I should be publicly beaten." Likewise, if people didn't get what they were due, he declared it was his fault. In that way he helped the Illustrious Ancestor to be worthy of High Heaven. So help me to do as my most illustrious forebear did, to achieve the best that the House of Shang can do and not just leave such an achievement to him. A prince without a good minister cannot rule. And a good minister without a good prince is no real use. So, now, sir, will you help me to be a worthy successor to my Ancestral King and thereby instruct the people in peaceful ways?'

Yue kowtowed and said, 'I will try to do as you ask. And in this way I will fulfil the will of the Son of Heaven.'

24

KING GAOZONG'S
SACRIFICE DAY

One day, when Gaozong was performing the ritual sacrifice, a pheasant appeared and it crowed at him.

Minister Zu Ji reacted to this by saying, 'If our State is to be united, first we have to communicate with the king.'

So it was that that he spoke up in front of the king, saying, 'When Heaven above seeks for unity amongst all the people below, it first looks at whether they are righteous people and then it bestows upon them either a long life or a short one.

'However, it is not Heaven that cuts short a person's life. It is what they have done themselves that determines this.

'Heaven would like to reform those who behave badly and fail to acknowledge their faults. But they are the kind of people who say, "What can I do anyway!"

'Indeed, the king's role has always been to care for the people and you are heir to those whom Heaven has favoured in the past. Honour your ancestors with your sacrifices but do not focus your attention just upon your own father.'

The king here is the last and most despised of all the Shang rulers – indeed, he has become the model of the corrupt, tyrannical ruler for China. King Zhou traditionally reigned from 1154 to his overthrow and the end of the Shang/Yin dynasty in 1122 BC. King Wen was the ruler of a small state to the west and was the founder figure but not the first ruler of the Zhou dynasty which traditionally ran from 1122 to 236 BC, though from the eighth century BC onwards this was only in name, not in any sense in reality.

25

THE LORD OF THE WEST CONQUERS LI

When King Wen, Lord of the West conquered the land of Li, Minister Zu Yi rushed to inform the king of the Yin.

'Son of Heaven,' he said. 'It is clear that Heaven wills the destruction of the dynasty of Yin. Having consulted sages and divination, none of them predicts good fortune for you. You cannot blame your Ancestral Kings of the past for any disregard for the people. You, and you alone, are the instrument of this downfall through your own wild lifestyle and indulgence. This is why Heaven has abandoned us, leaving us in such dire circumstances without even enough to eat.

'You have failed to understand the wishes of Heaven or to follow the proper laws. Throughout your land, all the people are hoping your dynasty will fall. They are asking, "Why hasn't Heaven punished them yet? Why has the Great Mandate not made this clear? What good is this present king?"'

'Indeed,' the king replied. 'Am I not dependent upon the Mandate of Heaven for my own life?'

'Indeed,' Zu Yi said back to him. 'How can you claim to still have the Mandate of Heaven when your manifold wickednesses are only too well known? Very soon the Dynasty of Yin will fall and you will be to blame. Can you not consider the significance of this condemnation and its impact upon your country?'

The nobility of this brother of the evil King Zhou and of the Principal Scholar highlights the corruption of the king himself. This is the last year of the Shang – traditionally 1123 BC.

26

THE VISCOUNT OF WEI

The Viscount was outspoken, and said:

'Scholars, great and small, this Yin dynasty
has now lost its right to rule over our land.
Our ancestors were appointed from on high
knowing what needed to be done, and how to do it.
But all that's been lost through drunkenness,
and the virtue of the past has been betrayed.

The people of Yin think it's fine
to perform crimes of daylight robbery and viciousness
no matter how great or small.
The nobles even encourage each other in this
and no one is ever challenged! But now
the common people are in revolt, and at last
the whole edifice is collapsing . . .

It's like someone who wants to cross a great river
who hasn't a hope of finding a ford or boat
– that's why we are facing ruin.'

He added:

'Scholars, we must be mad. You and your families
have fled and taken refuge in the countryside.
You haven't faced what is happening
so what are you going to do now?'

The Principal Scholar responded to him, saying:

'My Lord, Heaven is bringing disaster on us
and destroying this land of Yin!
So we have sunk into the mire of drunkenness.
There's no fear or incentive any longer
and the wisdom of the elders is despised.
Now the people are killing the sacred animals
meant for the deities, and eating them
and no one is penalized. This dreadful behaviour
is because they've been treated so appallingly,
and that's why they've become like this!

In truth, the responsibility is ours. Look at the poor,
they've given up all hope of salvation.

Now disaster is poised to come down
and I must acknowledge my part in this. When we fall,
I will never serve as a minister again.
So listen to me, my master.
Leave, as fast as you can – escape.
I did not serve you as well as I should have –
but now, listen to me – and run!
Otherwise we face complete annihilation.

We each have to make our own decision,
and we'll each have to answer for this to our ancestors,
but I have chosen to stay. My refuge is here.'

THE BOOK OF ZHOU

周 書

The Zhou dynasty ousted the Shang and this traditionally took place in 1122 BC. The dynasty ruled in theory until 221 BC, but in reality its days of power were over by 770 BC.

This marks the launch of the campaign by the Zhou against the Shang by the son of King Wen, King Wu (also known as Fa), and thus falls around 1123 BC. It is also referred to in the Yi Jing and in the Shi Jing.

27

THE GREAT VOW, PART I

It was in the spring of the thirteenth year that the great gathering of the clans took place on the border at Meng Jin. Here it was that the king spoke.

'My dear friends, drawn from the many states, and my officers – listen to what I am going to say and understand clearly my vow,' he said.

'Heaven and Earth are together the mother and father of all life. And of all creatures, human beings are the most intelligent. And the first amongst these become the rulers and as the rulers they are in effect the mother and father of the people.

'Now the Shang king, by the name of Zhou, has shown disrespect to Heaven Above and as a result has brought disaster on the people. He has become so lost in drink and lust that he has become a terrible tyrant. He has punished entire families, not just the actual criminal; he has favoured a few families by making key posts hereditary and his obsession with building himself luxurious palaces, vast pleasure complexes with lakes and water features, has been at the expense of you, the people. He has tortured the most loyal and good people and has cut open the bellies of pregnant women. It was Heaven's Will that my father should protect the Majesty of Heaven, but he was unable to finish this.

'This is why I, little child of his that I am, I who am called Fa, am thinking about the future of the ruler of the Shang very seriously with you today, my dear friends. Unfortunately King Zhou does not seem to wish to reform his ways. He sits by idly, ignoring the Ruler on High, the deities and the spirits, neglecting his ancestors and their temple and its rituals. As a consequence, thieves are getting away with the ritual food and objects. Despite all this, he continues to insist, "I have the people and I have the Mandate." He is without shame!

'Heaven gave the ordinary people rulers and advisors in order to protect them. When they are united, they can follow the Ruler on High in order that every part of the land is at peace. Now, whether we are responsible or not, who are we to go against the Will of Heaven?

'In looking for strength, let us also seek virtue; and in looking for virtue, let us also seek righteousness. King Zhou may have many ministers and countless officials, but none of them are agreed. By contrast, I have three thousand officials who are united in heart and mind.

'The sheer scale of Shang's wickedness is overwhelming and Heaven's Mandate has been given to us so we can destroy them. If I were to fail to carry out Heaven's desire, then my failure would be as great as Shang's. I, who am but a little child in all this, find myself deeply troubled night and day because I have inherited this great responsibility from my father.

'So, having made sacrifices to the Ruler on High and performed the correct rituals for the deities of the land, I will now lead us all in carrying out the instructions from Heaven. Heaven cares deeply for the people. What the people long for, Heaven means to give. So come now, help me, a simple man, to reform the world.

'This is the time and we must not waste it.'

28

THE GREAT VOW, PART II

On Wu Wu, the fifty-fifth day of the calendar cycle, the king stopped to the north of the river and gathered here his nobles and their troops. Reviewing them, the king made this vow.

'Indeed,' the king said.

'Pay attention, you armies of the Western lands, to what I am about to say. I have heard it said that those who are fortunate and do what is right find there are not enough hours in the day to achieve everything. Likewise, bad people doing what is not right find the same thing.

'Now, the Shang King Zhou determinedly walks the way of wickedness. He spurns the old and wise and consorts with wicked men instead. He is a drunken, violent oppressor and those below him follow his example. They compete and feud with each other and, imitating his bad example, plot against each other. The innocent people call out to Heaven and these terrible deeds are observed.

'Heaven is united in caring deeply for the people and therefore any ruler should fear Heaven. When Jie of the Xia dynasty no longer followed the unity of Heaven and instead spread poison to all people everywhere in the land, Heaven's Mandate was passed to Tang the Conqueror, who was given permission to end the Mandate of Xia. Today, the wickedness of King Zhou exceeds everything done by Jie, for he has spurned and dishonoured the good men and has ruled as a tyrant, oppressing those who have sought to give him good advice. Claiming he has the Mandate of Heaven, he does not feel the need to act with due respect, nor offer the proper sacrifices – indeed, he claims that his acts of oppression are therefore of no consequence.

'All this is exactly repeating what befell the king of the Xia because Heaven has chosen me to rule the people instead. Moreover, my hopes have been confirmed by the diviners' reading of the oracles, and the omens say now is the time to overthrow the Shang.

'King Zhou has vast numbers of men, but they lack a common concern or a shared virtue. Meanwhile, I have my own group of statesmen and they are all of a common mind and a shared virtue. He has his allies, but they are so unlike my own loyal men. What Heaven observes, my people observe. What Heaven notes, my people note. The representatives of the people are asking why I have so far done nothing. I am but a simple man, but now I must make my move. My army is ready and united, so now we will invade and capture this tyrant. What I am about to achieve will excel that of the Mighty Tang. To arms, my heroes! Do not underestimate him – fear his ability but remember also that his troops are frightened of him and they are wavering. Indeed, unite in your virtue; be of one heart and mind and together we will this day undertake that of which men will speak for generations to come.'

29

THE GREAT VOW, PART III

The very next day the king inspected his six battalions and
made this binding vow to them all:

'You of the Western Lands, my brave noblemen!
Heaven follows the Way of the Dao
so we know what its true nature is.

And, as you know, the Shang King Zhou
has wilfully neglected the Five Precepts,
behaving disgustingly and disgracefully.

So: Heaven has cut him off – because
he's utterly alienated his own people
and ignored his teacher!

Listen: he dissected the bare legs
of those who work deep in the paddy fields
and cut out for casual inspection
the hearts of the highest men!

His depravity has spread corruption
and desolation throughout the land.

He kowtows to the evil and dissolute,
throwing out the conscientious scholar!

The rituals for honouring the deities
and the ancestors have been abandoned,
instead he panders to the cruel whims
of his pleasure-seeking whores!

The Ruler on High has ordered punishment,
so will you stand with me, a simple man,
in fulfilling Heaven's decree?

The Ancient Ones had a saying:
Whoever comforts us is our prince,
whoever oppresses us is our enemy.

This pathetic wretch, Zhou, is your enemy
and the enemy of your ancestors, too,
because he has brought such misery.

For virtue to blossom, it has to be nurtured.
To deal with evil, it has to be rooted out.

And this is why I, a child, need your strength
 – the strength of all of you gathered here –
to abolish this monstrous enemy.

So, brave ones, let us stand firm
and see that this takes place!

Merit will follow bravery, and great reward,
but if you fail, then disgrace!

My father was like the sun and moon
who lit every corner of the Western lands.
This is why you've come to help the House of Zhou!

If we defeat King Zhou, that will not be my achievement
but that of my father.

But if King Zhou defeats us, it will fall on me,
child that I am, and unworthy.'

This is thought to have been constructed as a text for recitation and performance at the annual commemoration of the defeat of the Shang by the Zhou. It is likely that at these same celebrations the Yi Jing was also used to enhance the sense of the mystical, Heavenly inspired nature of the revolt and successful revolution.

30
THE VOW AT MU

It was just before dawn on the Jia Zi day – the first day – when the King of the Zhou came to the border with the Shang kingdom at the place called Mu. And here they all made their vow.

The king was carrying a battle-axe decorated with yellow in his left hand while in his right he held a white standard. This he brandished furiously, shouting, 'You have travelled far, you men of the Western Lands!

'My liege lords, ministers and officials; commanders of the hosts; commanders of the cavalry; commanders of the infantry; leaders of thousands and officers of hundreds,' he said to them all in welcome. 'You have come, all of you, from so many different regions and places. All of you raise your weapons of war and raise your shields as I declare this vow.'

Saying this, the king declared:

'The Ancient Ones say
The morning isn't heralded by a hen!
If it is, something is deeply wrong
in the household.

And it is. The Shang King Zhou
only pays attention to his women.
He dismisses the rituals of sacrifice.
He fails to honour his family line
choosing the dregs of the Empire instead,
criminals to a man!

Honours have been heaped on them,
and so they or it over the people.
Shang has become a place of evil!

So I, Fa, have been sent to punish him.
And now, today, be careful, men
not to advance more than six or seven steps
before you halt and make a line. Be strong!

And in the battle's heat
don't go beyond four or five strokes
or six or seven blows . . . before reforming.

Be true warriors! Imagine
you are tigers, you are panthers
be like bears, like angry bears!
Your fight is here on this border.

But don't kill those who surrender
bring them as allies free to join
those of you from the Western Lands.

Be brave because if you aren't
death will be your only reward!'

This traditionally is 1122 BC. The text here is very confused and we have sought to arrange it so as to make sense, but it is not an easy chapter of which to make logical and chronological sense.

31

THE END OF THE WAR

The moon returned on the Ren Chen day of the first month and early in the morning of the very next day, the king advanced from Zhou and attacked the Shang.

By the Wu Wu day the army had crossed the ford of Meng and by the next day were assembled on the borders of Shang in accordance with Heaven's Decree. It was early morning on the Jia Zi day when Zhou advanced with an army as vast as a forest. They gathered in the desert of Mu but they failed to attack my army. Instead, their front line attacked those behind them who then fled in confusion. So much blood was spilled, it flowed like a river. And so it was that all below Heaven was greatly pacified and the rule of Shang was overthrown and order restored. Qi was freed from prison and a proper mound built over the grave of Bi Gan. The ordinary people benefited from the wealth and we handed out the treasures of the Treasure House, known as the Stag Gallery. Grain was distributed from the store house and so it was that to the joy of everyone, magnificent gifts were given out across the land.

In the fourth month, when the moon was likewise new, the king came from Shang to Feng and silenced the tumult of war.

Now he could turn his attention to the issues of peace. His war horses went back to the south side of Mount Hua and his cattle were sent back to graze. This, more clearly than anything else, showed everyone that the war was over.

On the Ding Wei day he offered the ritual sacrifices in the
Ancestral Temple of the Zhou, surrounded by scurrying ministers anxious to please. Three days later, he restored the practice
of making burned offerings and thus made the great announcement that the war was over. As the moon waned, the princes of
the House from the many regions were appointed to their specific tasks, in order to fulfil what The Zhou wanted to happen.

'Indeed, my war host of nobles,' the king said. 'The Ancestor
King was responsible for founding our state by claiming this ter-
ritory. As you know, Noble Liu built upon the worthiness of the
Great King; King Shu laid the foundations; King Qi built up the
Royal House; while my father, my Royal Father, fulfilled all this
and as a result was given the Mandate of Heaven in order to
bring truth and peace to the land. The great states were in awe
and trembling of his vigour while the lesser states loved him for
his virtue. Nevertheless, after nine years, the task was still unfinished and it fell to me, the little child, to complete his task.'

The king loathed everything that Shang had done wrong and
this led him to make the following announcement to Heaven,
to the Noble Earth, to the sacred mountains and the Great River.

'I who now have the Way, Fa, the King of the Zhou
am ready to undertake the judgement on Shang!
This creature, known as Zhou, has failed the Way in all
        ways.
He's a gross dictator, oppressing everything under heaven,
especially his own people, and has become the worst of
        beings
surrounding himself with others of his kind . . . like a
        shoal of fish
as though they were all living like wild animals in a
        jungle!

Now I, child as I also am, surrounded by benevolent men
who revere the Ruler on High, have terminated his vile
        ways.
Both the civilized, and the wild tribes are ready to
        follow me!

Holding Heaven's Mandate, I attacked to the East
and brought peace to its good people, women and men
who brought me tribute of multi-coloured silks
honouring how the kings of Zhou are honoured by
    Heaven.
And so they have come to the great state of Zhou.

Now you, great deities, give me your blessing ,
so I can protect this multitude, and also bring to an end
your distress with us!'

The nobles were reorganized into the five official ranks and the land itself into three parts. Offices were awarded only to those who were worthy of them and able to carry them out properly. He laid down that the people must be taught the five principles and proper attention was to be restored to the food, rituals and worship associated with mourning. He valued truth and his righteousness shone forth. Virtue was rewarded and so too was merit. Then he settled upon his Throne, folded his hands and all below Heaven was properly governed.

This chapter is of fundamental importance as an articulation of ancient Chinese philosophy.

32
THE GREAT PLAN

It was at the time of his thirteenth annual sacrifice as king that he went to see the Viscount of Qi and said, 'Indeed, Viscount of Qi, Heaven's mysterious purpose has enabled the ordinary people to develop and prosper together in harmony. Yet I do not really understand how the ways of good governance were developed.'

The Viscount of Qi replied, 'Long ago, so I have heard, when Gun fought the Great Flood he upset the Five Elements. This provoked the Ruler to great anger and as a result he did not share with him the Great Plan in its Nine Sections. Because of this, the fundamental principles were lost and Gun was forced into exile, where he died. It fell to Yu to rise up and take on the mantle of his task, whereupon Heaven shared with Yu the Great Plan and its Nine Sections.

'And so it was that everything was once again in order.

'The first of the Nine is the Five Elements
the second is respect for the Five Conducts
the third is taking care of the Eight Regulations
the fourth is details of the Annual Records
the fifth is perfecting Princely Rule
the sixth is proper use of the Three Virtues
the seventh . . . the Exploration of Uncertainty
the eighth, the purposeful use of Understanding
the ninth the careful use of the Five Good Fortunes
– with a respect for the Six Extremes.

The Five are: water, fire, wood, metal and earth.
Water pours down; fire blazes and rises
wood is either crooked or straight
metal does as it's commanded
earth sprouts crops.

What soaks becomes salty,
what burns becomes bitter,
what is crooked or straight becomes sour,
what is hard but melts becomes acrid,
what is sown and reaped is delicious!

The Five Conducts are:
demeanour, speech, perceiving, hearing, thinking.
The essence of demeanour is respect
of speech – reason
of perception – clarity
of hearing – comprehension
and of thinking – perception.

And so respect creates reverence
reason creates order
clarity creates wisdom
understanding creates possibilities
– and perception creates the sage.

'The Eight Regulations are agriculture; trade; sacrifices; public affairs; education; justice; hospitality and finally the military.

'The five key astrological aspects of the Annual Records are the year; the month; the day; the stars and planets and finally the calendar.

'Perfect princely rule occurs when the prince seeks perfection in his bestowing of the Five Good Fortunes, sharing these with all the people. In return the people will become defenders of this and will trust the prince. The people will therefore never plot or the statesman be so self-centred as would otherwise be the case and the ruler will achieve his highest ambitions and status.

'Those who refrain from doing what is wrong and show ability should be looked upon with favour. Those who are not necessarily perfect in behaviour yet are also not criminal in intent should be told off in order that they can improve. Bless with good fortune those who are peaceful and virtuous. In time, these men will all come together in the service of princely perfection. Do not harm the weak and vulnerable, but be wary of the high and cunning. The country will prosper if you encourage men of ability who can exercise authority. Properly reward the most judicious officials and encourage them. If you do not do this, you will build up resentment in their households and this will swiftly turn into corruption. Those who do not love virtue must never be rewarded because this will only increase their appetite for corruption and you will be held responsible for this.

> 'Without diversion, without ambivalence
> follow the Royal Model.
> Without pursuing your own desire
> walk the way of the Royal Path.
> Without resentment,
> be guided by the Royal Path.
> Without factions, without prejudice
> the Royal Path is smooth, is easy.
> Without prejudice, without breaking away
> the Royal Path is level, is straight.
> Without stupidity, without bias
> the Royal Way is true and appropriate.
> Seeing such excellence,
> follow it!'

The king said, 'The model of such princely perfection should be taught as the true principle to guide the Emperor as it guides Heaven. When the people act like this, then they draw close to the glory of the Son of Heaven and say, "The Son of Heaven is like both father and mother to the peoples and this is why he is the king of everything that lives." '

The Three Virtues are integrity, firm government and

moderation. In times of peace and happiness, use integrity; in times of rebellion, use firm government; while in times of well-being and contentment, use moderation. When dealing with the uncertain, use firm government; while with the bright, use moderation. It is the prerogative of the prince to use the wealth of the kingdom to bestow blessings in order to inspire both dread and awe. This is not the role of the statesman. If they do, this is bad for the Family and is dangerous for the country. Having the wrong kind of person in such a role corrupts and leads the people astray.

'Exploration of Uncertainty. Appoint diviners to consult the oracles – be that the turtle or the milfoil. But ensure they do this properly. By this they can predict rain, mist, fog or bad weather and these readings can be seen to be genuine and evoke contrition. These seven – five are given by the tortoise and two by the milfoil – are all worthy of careful attention. When it comes to appointing good people, three people should be consulted and follow any two who agree.

'If you are really not sure, examine your own heart on the matter and then your ministers and then the ordinary people before you go to ask the tortoise or the yarrow stalks.

'If they all agree: that is to say
the people, the tortoise shell and the yarrow stalks –
this is truly remarkable, and you will be fine
as will your family; you will be blessed.

If you, the tortoise and the yarrow stalks agree
but not the ministers and the people –
you will still be all right.

If the ministers agree with the tortoise and the yarrow stalks
but you and the people disagree –
it may still be OK.

If you and the tortoise agree, but the yarrow stalks
ministers and people do not –
then this is OK for internal affairs
– but not good for external ones.

If the tortoise and the yarrow stalks agree
but you, the ministers and people do not
then the *status quo* will be safe
but don't try and undertake new actions.

Means of Understanding: rain, sun, heat, cold, wind
and the seasons. If they combine at the right time
then everything grows in abundance. But if one
is dominant, this is not good – and likewise
if one is weak or insignificant, this is bad too.

This is what we call *auspicious relationships*
respect brings appropriate showers
good government brings bright sunshine
wisdom brings the right amount of heat,
good counsel brings necessary coolness
and wisdom brings the breathing wind.

But there are the inauspicious relationships!
Wildness brings flooding – foolishness, drought
selfishness brings heat waves, rashness bitter cold
while stupidity
                ushers in storms . . .

He said, 'The king's behaviour shapes the fate of the whole
year; that of a minister shapes the whole month; that of local
officials shapes a whole day. If everything is done properly
throughout the year, through every month and every day, then
all crops will grow well, the government will be wise and only
those who are competent will be appointed. As a result, every
household will be prosperous and at peace. But if the proper
order is not obeyed, and as a result the year, the month and day
are disturbed, then all crops will fail, the government will not

be good, the able will go unrecognized and all households will be distressed. The people are like the stars. Some stars love the wind; some stars love the rain. The sun and moon give rise to winter and summer. The travels of the moon amongst the stars bring the wind and rain.

'The Five Good Fortunes are called, firstly, long life; secondly, wealth; thirdly, well-being and peace; fourthly, love of virtue; and finally, a good end to life. The Six Extremes are called tragic death; secondly, illness; thirdly, sorrow; fourthly, poverty; next, evil; and finally, weakness.'

33

THE HOUND OF LÜ

After the conquest of Shang, it was once again possible to travel along the main roads. This meant it was also feasible for the nine barbarian peoples and the eight wild peoples from the Western tribe of Lü to send a huge hound as tribute. To mark this, the Grand Guardian composed a poem called 'The Hound of Lü'. It says:

> A wise king pays attention to his virtue:
> and then the rough barbarians on every side
> come to acknowledge his rule.

> They come from near and far
> proffering their wares –
> clothes, food, vessels.

> The king displays them as signs of his virtue,
> and as long as they're true to their duties
> he awards them to the local governors.

> The treasures with their gems are shared
> with relatives who administer the territories –
> which further coheres them.

> Such people accept these
> because they see them
> as the fruits of virtue!

Real virtue doesn't despise anyone.
But if a ruler insults his leaders,
they won't trust him

and if he abuses the trust
of the ordinary people
they won't support him, either.

So long as you are not just
preoccupied with sensual things,
then all will go well.

Toying with people ruins virtue,
playing around compromises your focus
 – you must always follow the Way.

What you say should tally with it too
because who you really are
will be visible if you don't waste your time
on trivial pursuits.

Never ignore those who are worthy
nor value the strange above the useful.
Hold to this, and the people will be fine.

Strange dogs and horses shouldn't be prioritized
likewise strange birds and creatures
shouldn't be encouraged here.

Disdain alien things . . .
if you give them no value
then strangers will be impressed!

Only praise what is real,
then the people will be at peace.

And never fail to be conscious,
day in and day out.
Always pay attention to the small things
otherwise virtue's potential will founder.

In building a mound nine fathoms high,
all it takes to fail
is to let one bucket of earth slip!

Try genuinely to live like this,
and your people will feel safe
your dynasty will outlast time.

The first appearance of the Duke of Zhou, also called Dan, who now dominates the remainder of the book. He was the fourth of King Wen's ten sons (of which the current king is one, the 'Two Dukes' are two others and Guanshu is another). The Duke of Zhou is considered in Chinese thought to be the model of a Confucian noble. This begins the sequence in which the Zhou dynasty takes over from the Shang.

34
THE GOLDEN CHEST

Two years after the final fall of the Shang, the king fell seriously ill. The Two Dukes decided to urgently seek the advice of the oracle. The Duke of Zhou urged them not to disturb the Ancestors of the King and said that he would deal with this himself. So he built three altars on an earth terrace with a further one to the south, facing north, and it was here that he stood. On the altars lay the jade discs. In his hands he held the badges of office and then he invoked the Three Ancestor Kings – Tai, Ji and Wen.

The Recorder wrote down everything and the Duke said:

'Please be informed that your Royal Heir, the King, is seriously ill. He places his trust on you Three Ancestor Kings. This son, me, standing here, trusts that the case will be presented to Heaven. And I trust that should anyone have to die, it will be me, Dan, instead. My wish is to take up this burden myself. The kindness I show is because my ancestors were virtuous. I have so many talents and skills, which means I could really be a good servant to the spirits and deities. Your heir does not have these talents and skills. So, to speak frankly, in comparison with me he would be of little use to the spirits and deities.

'It is the will of the Heavenly Emperor that the king rule

over all the land. And that from him will come future generations who will rule likewise. This is why he is venerated by all
the people in the country. It isn't possible that this Heavenly
Mandate will fall nor that the Great Ancestor should fail to
have a dynasty that lasts for ever.

'This is why I have come before the Great Oracle. If you will
tell me my fate, I will take up my symbols of power and return
home to await whatever happens. If, however, you do not
reveal my fate to me, I will lay aside all these symbols of
authority.'

Saying this, he cast the oracle three times. And all three cast-
ings said the same thing. Then he used a key to open the Chest
of the Oracles and this too said the same thing.

'The king's life is not in danger,' the duke then reported
back. 'I, just a simple ordinary man, having sought the advice
of the Three Ancestor Kings, can assure you this is so. As for
me, I will await whatever blessing comes.'

The duke placed the records of the oracles in the Golden
Chest and the very next day the king recovered.

When much later the king died, Guanshu and his younger
brothers spread malicious rumours throughout the land that
the Duke of Zhou would prove to be a serious problem for the
young king.

The Duke of Zhou turned to the Two Dukes, and told them
he did not wish to act as the regent for the young king as he
feared that he would not be able to undertake this properly,
and thus could never stand proudly before the Ancestor King.
He then left for the east of the country, where he stayed for two
years until those responsible for this subversion were revealed.
In thanksgiving the duke composed an ode called 'The Owl',*
which he presented to the king. The king did not try to incrim-
inate the duke.

Then, just before the harvest, at the time of the Great
Autumn Festival, Heaven sent a mighty storm. With thunder
and lightning and wind, it beat down the harvest and uprooted

---

* The owl was seen as a hunter, preying upon innocent victims – like those
who disturbed and robbed the Royal House.

great trees. This terrified everyone, and the king and his mighty officers went, in full regalia, to examine the Records in the Golden Chest.

When they opened them, they discovered the account of the Duke of Zhou's offer to take the place of King Wu; to suffer his potentially fatal illness himself, and thus save the life of the old king.

The Two Dukes and the king, surrounded by their many officials, asked the Recorder about this. He replied saying, 'This is true but the Duke ordered us not to say anything about this to anyone.'

Holding the Record, the king wept and said, 'We need no further divination for us to understand how dedicated the Duke of Zhou is to the well-being of our Royal House. But because of our foolishness and youth, we did not understand this until today. This explains why Heaven has manifested its anger, so we will discover the true virtue of the Duke of Zhou. Now it is time for me, a mere stripling, to go and meet him, for this is how things should be done in both my Household and my kingdom.'

So the king went to the borderlands. Heaven sent rain and wind which enabled the harvest to recover. The Two Dukes ordered the people to replace or replant the great trees and in the end the harvest that year was exceptional.

The new king here is King Cheng, the son of King Wu, who speaks out against rebels especially from the remainder of the Shang dynasty ministers who have joined with some of the disgruntled other sons of King Wen.

35

THE GREAT ANNOUNCEMENT

The new king declared:

'Listen. I am going to make a major announcement to you, you leaders of the many states, and you, my officials. Things right now are pretty dire. Heaven has, almost without cessation, placed a curse upon my House and I have to face up to this now. Although I have immense power and am responsible for making major decisions which directly affect the well-being of the people, fundamentally I lack experience. To be honest, I can say that frankly I have really very little understanding of what the Mandate of Heaven actually means.

'I am like an innocent child who is trying to wade across a deep river and who knows it's stupid but has no option but to carry on. I have tried to continue the work of my beloved forebears in the way they lived, and true to the Mandate they had received. While I really have tried, I have to acknowledge that Heaven has punished me, despite my best efforts.

'The previous king, may he rest in peace, left me the Great Treasure Tortoise Shell. Through it, Heaven can speak to me words of wisdom and understanding – which will reveal its Will. The oracle has spoken, saying that there will be serious troubles in the Western Lands and that the tribes there will be rebellious. The State of Yin has already been shattered into pieces and yet these people now plan to seize control. This is despite the fact that Heaven has already punished the country and all the people are disturbed and perplexed. The rebel leader says, "I will take it back" and now plans to marginalize our people once again.

'This pointless, stupid plan emerged one day and then the very next day ten leaders came forth from my people to assist me in rousing them to action. I have consulted the oracle and it has said that this undertaking will be successful.

'So, my princes, officials, officers and administrators, because of this auspicious oracle, we are now going to attack the Yin and punish them for their crimes. I know this will not be popular. All of you, of whatever rank, will say this is too great an undertaking and that it will disturb the people. You will also complain that this idea comes from the King's Palace egged on by the princes and that no one else wants this. It is a view held by the old as well as the young. It is being said that this is not actually in accord with the oracle.

'Being so young, I have of course pondered upon this and want to say this to you. There is no doubt that this action will harm the weak and vulnerable, but I have inherited the designs of Heaven and I have therefore taken on this demanding task. I cannot just worry about myself and my own well-being. Instead, you, my princes, and all the rest of you must advise me. Reflect on the fact that you should really say to me, "Do not leave unfinished the labours of your father, may he rest in peace."

'How can I, simple, little me, ignore the Mandate that comes from the Ruler on High? Heaven blessed my father the king, may he rest in peace, and raised up our humble State of Zhou. The oracle spoke to the king and from this flows all that has been commanded since. Through this we know Heaven is with the people, so I have no option but to follow the dictate of the oracle. Indeed, Heaven's insight means that you too must work with me to fulfil this awesome task.'

The king continued, saying, 'You, you were all my father's allies and advisors, so you know from the past that this was the great undertaking of the king, may he rest in peace. Heaven has shut itself off from us and this is deeply troubling. I must

therefore start from that fact and realize that I have no other
option but to take up the task of my worthy forebear. I want to
convince you, my princes, to join me in this great venture.

> 'I know Heaven supports this because I see it in the
>   attitudes of the people.
> So who am I to hesitate?
> Who am I not to finish this task
> which was started by that Man of Peace?
>
> The people are disturbed by Heaven
> as if they were suffering from some illness.
> So who am I not to finish this task
> which was started by that Man of Peace?'

The king then said: 'When I first spoke about this, I told you,
having reflected deeply about it all, that this would be difficult.

> 'It is like trying to build a house based upon a father's
>   blueprint.
> But if the son cannot even get round to building the main
>   hall,
> how likely is he to try and put a roof over it all?
> Or it can be compared to when a father ploughs the field
> but his son can't even be bothered to sow the seeds.
> And if he can't be bothered to sow the seeds,
> then he is even less likely to bother to harvest the crops.
> I think it is highly unlikely that such a hardworking
>   father
> will say of such a son
> that he will protect the family's inheritance.
> This is why I must undertake this great task
> which was the intention of the Man of Peace, the King.
> I must fulfil the Mandate.
> Imagine.
> If a father or elder brother saw the younger son being
>   attacked,
> would he stop the people from coming to help?

'Indeed,' the King said, 'rise up to this challenge, you princes and leaders.

'Because there are ten leaders
Who, understanding the Will of the Ruler on High,
obey it, this state will achieve levels of magnificence.

When all this began,
you did not reject the decrees,
so why now,
when Heaven has punished the Zhou
would you choose to do so?

The rebels are gathering to attack our House
and yet you don't seem to have grasped
what the Will of Heaven is.

Look. Heaven is pruning the Yin bit by bit
like a gardener.
In which case,
how could I not undertake a similar task
in my own garden?
Heaven has shown without doubt
that it supports the labours of the Man of Peace,
the King.
Am I likely to either ignore the oracle
or the example of the Man of Peace?
The King who protected our entire land?
The auspicious auguries of the oracle
support this venture to the East.
There can be no question about this being the Mandate
    of Heaven.
The oracle has spoken.'

Wei is the same person as in chapter twenty-six. He is the senior surviving member of the royal household of Shang and as such must take up responsibility for maintaining the worship of his ancestors so that the new dynasty of Zhou does not offend the ancestors.

36
THE COMMISSION TO THE VISCOUNT OF WEI

The king spoke to the eldest son of the King of Yin and appointed him to oversee the rites and rituals due to his ancestors. He said:

> 'Follow the example of your ancient ones,
> the virtuous ones,
> for I can see you are a worthy man
> like your revered ancestors.
> Therefore
> I appoint you to conduct the correct rituals and protect the relics.
> You will be a guest in my Household,
> a friend to the State
> and this will last for generation after generation.
> Indeed,
> your ancestor Tang the Conqueror
> had the Mandate of Heaven bestowed upon him;
> he was so sagacious, respectful and profound
> Heaven's Emperor chose him.
> He reassured the people and defeated the rebels.
> Everything he undertook was a success;

his virtue was renowned throughout the land.
Your role is to continue this
by highlighting his example.
You have long had a reputation of being loved by the
     deities
and by the people
because you are faithful in fulfilling your duties.

'The Ruler on High delights in the united efforts and reverence of the people. It is because of all of this that I now appoint
you to be the High Noble of the East.

'Go forth with reverence and share your instructions.
Respect the role you have and the symbols of your Mandate
and in this way you will support the Royal House.
Add to the renown of your honourable ancestors;
be an inspiration to the people.
In this way
you will support me,
simple man that I am,
in maintaining virtue from generation to generation.

'By being an example to all the other states you will help
ensure that my State of Zhou is never troubled. Indeed. Go, be
well and never ignore what I have willed.'

Prince Kang is the ninth son of King Wen and is also called Feng. This is a confused chapter and it is not entirely clear for whom the Duke of Zhou is speaking.

37
ANNOUNCEMENT TO KANG

It was in the third month, when the moon was waning, that the foundation stones of the great new city were laid by the Duke of Zhou. The new city was in the eastern part of the country known as Luo. The people came rejoicing from near and far, with leaders and ministers from so many states joining together to honour the Zhou. The Duke of Zhou, urging true care and consideration, speaking for the king, announced the following major laws.

'Leaders of the princes,' he said. 'My younger brother Feng. Our honourable forebear, King Wen, was a wise and virtuous leader who was careful in the administration of punishments. He was always respectful to the poor and defenceless; he chose only people who were able; he respected the respectable and frightened those who needed to be scared. Because of this, the people trusted him. It was from humble beginnings that he, helped by just a few others, founded our state.

'Over time, all of the Western Lands came under his benevolent sway. The Ruler on High heard about him and was pleased. And so it came to pass that Heaven bestowed the Mandate upon King Wen, granting permission to attack Yin. Blessed by this Mandate, he was able to win, and all the leaders and their people came under his sway. Then the elder brother tried to take over and this is why you, Feng the younger, are here in the Western Lands.

'The king has commented that you, Feng, you should indeed think about all of this. Because how you rule the people now will be contrasted with how closely this follows the model established by King Wen. Listen to what people say about his virtue, and about that of the First King of Yin and follow their examples in understanding how to rule the people. In similar fashion, follow the example of the ancient wise ones of Shang so that your heart will be attuned to their model. Learn from the wise kings of old and through this protect the well-being of the people. By upholding the Heavenly virtues you can fulfil the Royal Mandate you have been given.

'To this the king has added that you, Feng the Younger, should indeed know that being a ruler is like suffering from an illness. So be cautious. Fear of Heaven instils respect. While the machinations of the powerful are often only too visible, those of the ordinary people are less so.

'Move ahead, but also reflect.
If you do not desire ease and comfort,
then you will be able to rule the people.
There is the old saying that I have heard:

Dissatisfaction is not caused by great issues;
Nor it is primarily caused by minor concerns.
It is essentially caused
by how a ruler manages things,
Wisely or otherwise,
And by what degree he commits himself –
Or fails so to do.

'Your role, little one, is to support and increase the Royal power and to protect the people of Yin. Then they will support the king and by obeying the Mandate of Heaven, they will be able to become a new people.

'Moreover, Feng, be enlightened in your use of punishments. If someone commits a minor crime but does so deliberately and persistently, never mind how minor, execute him.

'If someone commits a major crime, but does not do so deliberately but by accident or mistake, and confesses to this, then do not execute him.

'Listen, Feng. The people will work together in unison if you always do the right thing because this will enlighten them. The people will cast away wrongdoing as if it were sickness, and as a result, there will be peace and unity. It's as if they are just children. Remember, Feng, it is not your role alone to punish or execute. Nor must you act alone in deciding upon punishments such as mutilation of the nose or ear.

'When dealing with external affairs, follow the rules of Yin. They are appropriate for such cases. Before making a decision, reflect for five or six days, maybe even longer – say, ten days, and then after a while, perhaps even as long as three months, make your decision.

'Follow the calendar of the Yin in terms of when to have legal proceedings. Never decree death according to your own views or whims, but according to what is right. Follow this and you can justly claim you did what was right. I cannot stress enough that you must only do what is right and proper.

'Prepare yourself. Even though you are young, you have a good heart. Follow my example which you can see set before you.

'Remember, everyone hates those who rob, steal, are rebels, murderers, looters and those who laugh at death.

'Feng. While everyone loathes such people, the worst of all are those who are unfilial and unfriendly.

'If a son offends his father and wounds him to the heart, the father will no longer be able to love his son and this in turn will hurt the son.

'A younger brother who does not honour Heaven and as a result fails to respect his older brother will cause his older brother to forget all that tradition has taught him and he will despise his younger brother.

'If we who are in charge fail to act against those who break the rules, then the patterns established by Heaven will be ignored or even worse will disappear.

'I recommend that as in the days of King Wen, you punish swiftly, sternly and without mercy.

'Those who act so badly must be punished severely. And if this is the general case, how much more so should officials in charge of teaching and order be punished if they promote dissent and peddle falsehoods just so they can be popular.

'Even worse are those who do nothing to ensure that the life of the ruler runs smoothly.

'It is these kinds of people who are the wickedest because they spread evil. I loathe them and you are to deal swiftly with them and execute them.

'If any of you assembled here, you princes and ministers, are unable to control your own households, your minor officials or your external affairs, without terrifying or abusing them, then by such actions you greatly undermine the authority of the Royal Mandate. This is against the true virtue of authority. You, above all, must follow the law and ensure the people are happy and prosperous. King Wen was such an example of respect and care that the people were at ease and felt able to do anything. Follow this and I, simple man that I am, will be content.

'Feng, you can help the people to prosperity and unity, but you need to reflect upon this. For example, I like to think about the virtue of the Kings of Yin and how this led to the well-being of the people. As the people now expect leadership, if we fail to lead they are not capable of taking charge themselves.

'Feng, let me tell you what I have learned from the Ancient Ones.

'Use virtue when deciding what is the appropriate punishment.

> 'Today the people are troubled;
> they are disturbed in their hearts and minds;
> this despite our best attempts to lead them properly.
> Frankly this is not working.

'When I reflect upon the reprimand that Heaven has sent upon me, I have no grounds for complaint because Heaven hears the report of offences committed, whether they are big or small is of no consequence.

'Listen, Feng.
Listen to me.
Always show reverence;
never cause gossip;
do not listen to bad advice nor behave badly.
Take time to consider what is true and significant; be
        guided by virtue.
Remain calm;
study virtue;
plan ahead.

'By these moderate steps you will be able to guide the people. They will then be content and therefore will not blame you or try to overthrow you.

'Indeed, you are young, Feng, and so you must understand that the Mandate can change. Ponder on this because I don't want to have to remove it from you.

'So, be wise;
do as I have told you;
follow my advice,
then you will govern your people well.

'Finally the king has said, "Go to it, Feng. Do not ignore the ritual responsibilities and pay attention to what I have said. Then the people of Yin will be loyal to your Household for generations to come."'

This continues the pronouncements to Feng, the ninth son of King Wen. It is not only historically interesting, but comments on a problem which afflicts China to this day.

38

THE PRONOUNCEMENT ON DRINKING

'Make it clear,' the king said to Feng. 'Make this major pronouncement clear to the people of the former capital of Yin. When your revered father King Wen founded the kingdom in the Western Lands, he made a pronouncement to all the officials and their assistants in all the states. It was a warning to those hard-working people. Remember, he warned, that the ritual wine has been set aside as Heaven has directed. But now Heaven punishes us because the people have become confused and lost their virtue all because they are now sunk in drunkenness. Whether on a grand scale or a lesser scale, the evils of drunkenness can destroy a state. This is why King Wen instructed the young, the officials and their officers not to indulge in regular drinking bouts. Wine should only be served for use in the proper rituals when, guided by virtue, there could be no excuse for drunkenness.

"My people, teach the young to be content to enjoy what the earth produces itself. As a result, their hearts and minds will be at peace. Let them listen carefully to the instructions of their elders so that the young will see that whether an action of virtue is great or small, they are all in essence the same.

"You who live here, gather in the harvest, work hard and in this way honour and serve your forebears and leaders. With the means you have at hand, oxen and carts, start trading abroad.

In this way you will be able to serve your elders and when you are able to care properly for your parents, making them happy, then and only then celebrate with wine.

"Now listen all of you, officials, officers, nobles, listen to my instructions. You may drink wine and celebrate with good food but only when you have done all that is necessary for the well-being of your elders and your ruler. Let it first be said of you that you pay attention to your own behaviour, choosing the middle path of virtue and undertaking all the proper rituals. Then you can go ahead and party. If you conduct yourselves like this, then you really will be ministers worthy of the king and Heaven will reward you because of your virtue. Nor will you ever be forgotten within the Royal Household."

'Feng, when the ministers, princes and young people of our Western Lands followed the teachings of King Wen, they did not get drunk. This is why I have now been given the Mandate to rule Yin.

'Feng, I have heard it said that the wise kings of Yin taught the people to revere Heaven. Because of this, the ordinary people themselves reflected this virtue and wisdom. From the time of Tang, right down to the time of the Emperor Yi, all the kings followed this example, as did their ministers. They would never dare to indulge themselves, let alone go drinking. This applied as much to those out on the wilder frontiers as well as those close to the Court – high or low, they would never dream of going drinking. Not only was this never in their minds, but frankly, they never had the time either for such frivolities. They were too busy helping the king show forth and increase his virtue. Which was why they were all revered.

'Sadly, I also heard it said recently that the last of these kings was a drunkard, with the result that the people did not know what he wanted them to do. Even when his actions stirred up resentment, he nevertheless pursued his debauched lifestyle. Watching him sink deeper and deeper into indulgence and alcoholism, the people lost all respect and were greatly troubled in their hearts and minds. He so abandoned himself to alcohol, never ever trying to recover or stop, that he became lost. So much so that he did not fear even death itself. His behaviour infected the capital of the Shang itself so that even when the kingdom of the Yin was invaded, he didn't care. He never even tried to act virtuously, not even to perform the correct rituals so that Heaven might hear him. The leaders became drunkards and the people hated him and Heaven noted all this. Which is why Heaven punished without mercy the Yin because of this disgraceful behaviour. Heaven itself did not initiate this but it responded to the distress of the people.

'Feng, I really don't want to go on about this other than to quote the old saying:

' "Do not look on water to truly see yourself, but look instead at what others reflect back to you of yourself."

'So, now Yin has lost the Mandate – and you will understand why I draw this analogy, in order to try and help restore peace and unity. All I would add is that you should strictly enforce a ban on drunkenness on all the officials of Yin – all of them – whoever they are, whether nobles, ministers, officers, those with responsibility for all aspects of the life of the State, of the military, of the law. Furthermore, I instruct you that if you hear of people getting together to drink, then you trap them and send them here to me in Zhou. And I will execute them. If, however, a minister has been led into drunkenness, then it may not be necessary to execute him. Instead we should try and educate and reform them instead. This cannot be put more clearly. I will execute anyone who disobeys. I, this man alone, will show no pity nor be swayed by any plea. I will just put them to death.

'Feng,' the king ended up by saying. 'Pay constant attention to my warning. If you fail to maintain order amongst your ministers, the people will sink into debauchery.'

*The final pronouncement to Feng but fused with general minis-
terial advice. The 'right stuff' refers to the wood to be used
when making good furniture.*

39
THE RIGHT STUFF

The king said to Feng:

'It takes a really good statesman to understand not just the
people themselves, but also the ministers and the great families,
and to be able to bring them into unity of intention.

'When you issue your instructions, you need to make sure
that there is no misunderstanding. You should say, "I have
many who assist me, ministers, for example, of war, civil
affairs, education and many others. Be assured that I will never
execute anyone without due cause."

'To encourage respect, show respect.

'So, for example, with some traitors and criminals, murderers and rebels – you should pardon them because then the
people will see that this is how a prince behaves. Similarly, pardon some of those who have attacked and harmed others.
When a king appoints the investigators in order to deal with
these sorts of problems, this is so as to reassure the people that
they are properly governed. He commands that the people
should never be harmed or oppressed, and that the weak and
destitute should be respected. Never waver in your concern for
the well-being of the people. When a king gives his orders to his
princes and their followers, what should his command be? It
must always be for the well-being of the people. This was how
the kings of old behaved and their investigators followed suit.

'Imagine you are managing a farm,' he added. 'The ground

has been dug, so now it is time to build the boundaries and the ditches.

'Or you could compare it to building a house. The walls are up and now you need to plaster them and put a roof on.

'Or maybe it is more like making furniture – you need the right stuff to start with and then you add whatever paint you need – such as red, for example.

'The Ancestor Kings took care about how they spread the light of their virtue. They took care to nurture and develop their relationships with their officials and as a result all the states sent them tribute. These signs of friendship came from across the land. Because they respected his virtuous rule, they were content to honour him by bringing their tributes. Imperial Heaven gave this kingdom and its people to the Ancestor King. This is why Your Majesty will be able to pacify and restore both this land and its rebellious people – because of your virtue. This will be a cause of rejoicing for our Ancestors who were first awarded the Mandate of Heaven.

'So, study this and reflect upon it. If you are successful, your descendants will rule for Ten Thousand years as the true protectors of the people.'

Grand Protector Shao is thought to be one of King Wen's sons and was given prime responsibility with Zhou to find a site for the new capital city. Creating a new capital especially for a new dynasty was the custom and involved extensive divination to ensure it was an auspicious site.

40

THE PRONOUNCEMENT OF SHAO

On the Yi Wei day in the second month, which fell six days after the full moon, the king left Zhou early in the morning and travelled to Feng.

On the third day of the third month, after the rise of the new moon, the Grand Protector Shao had gone to inspect the site at Luo, before the arrival of the Duke of Zhou.

On the Wu Shen day, three days later, the oracle was consulted about where the new city should be built. The augury was good, so the plans were laid out for this site.

It was three days after that, that the Grand Protector Shao led the people of Yin in preparing the site which lay at the junction of the Lo and Yellow Rivers.

By the fifth day this was finished.

On the following day, the Duke of Zhou came in the morning to Luo to inspect the plans for the new capital in detail.

Three days later, he performed the ritual sacrifices of two bulls, and the following day he performed the proper ritual sacrifices to the Earth God, offering a bull, a goat and a pig.

Seven days later, in the morning, the Duke of Zhou issued his written commands to all the people and their leaders, who upon receiving them rose up together to undertake this labour.

The Great Protector went to where the princes of the chief Houses were gathered and, accepting their tributes, he brought them to the Duke of Zhou, saying:

'I kowtow to you and I present them to you, my Duke, as if to the king himself. Through your pronouncements, order will be established amongst the Yin.

> 'Indeed, the Emperor of Heaven,
> the Ruler on High,
> has decided to alter the fate of this great Kingdom of
>   Yin, in favour of the eldest son.

> This Mandate,
> which our King has received,
> is a mixed blessing.
> It can be the cause
> of great happiness;
> it can be the cause
> of great anxiety;
> he has no option.
> He has to reverently obey.

'While Heaven has terminated the Mandate to Yin, nevertheless there are still of course their sage Ancestor Kings who dwell in Heaven. Sadly, it was their successors and their people who, having the Mandate, nevertheless began to behave badly, banishing the wise and instead bringing in oppressors.

'The downtrodden people, desperate to protect their women and children, raised their cry to Heaven itself. When they tried to flee, they were captured. However, Heaven had heard their cry and had compassion on the people throughout the land. As a result, the Mandate was given to our forebears, which is why the king must be the very model of virtue itself.

'Going back in time, we can see how the founder of the Xia was guided by Heaven and as a result we can see how the authority to rule passed down to his descendants because they were obedient to the Will of Heaven. Now time has passed, and over time the right to the Mandate was lost.

'The same thing happened with the Founder of the Yin. In the beginning Heaven guided the Yin and their descendants were blessed because they lived in accord with the Mandate of Heaven. But their descendants later squandered everything.

'Now our young king has ascended to the Throne. He must not neglect the elders and those people who have true experience, otherwise how will he come to understand the virtue of the ancient ones who themselves were guided by Heaven? Indeed, the king may be just a youth, but he is the chosen son who is expected to unite the ordinary people. He must be always alert to the dangers that confront the people; he must not fail to do this.

'So, let the king come as the Ruler on High wills, to rule this central land,' Dan said.

'By building this great city, he will be seen as a worthy counterpart of the Emperor of Heaven. He will make sacrifices to the spirits in Heaven and on Earth and then he will rule benevolently from this middle place. By the king ruling well and truly honouring and respecting the Mandate, the people will stay happy.

'The king must start by bringing the officials of Yin under his jurisdiction and making sure they are in line with the actions and decisions of our ministers of Zhou. If this happens, they will be of use daily and if the king does this he will show that he acts virtuously.

'I must not ignore the lessons of history –
the fates of the Xia and Yin dynasties.
I must not just say,
"The Xia had the Mandate of Heaven for many, many
      years."
But neither must I say,
"It was inevitable that it did not last."

'What I do know is that through lack of attention to virtue, it did not last as long as it should.

'Likewise, I know that I must not say:
"The Yin were supposed to have the Mandate of Heaven for many more years."

'Nor can I say:

"It could not last."

'However, the truth is that through a lack of virtue and respect, it ceased long before its time and the Mandate was lost.

'The king has now received the Mandate, the very one that these two dynasties had and lost. I think he should take note of the past but also have proper respect for their virtues as well.

'Actually, it is not that different from bringing up a child. So much of the child's intelligence is determined not just by what has been decreed but also by the impact of their early life.

'This is why Heaven has decreed insight to him.

'Will he be destined to have good fortune or bad?
To live for many years or not?
I have no idea.
What I do know
is that this is all just the beginning.

'Starting fresh in this new city, the king must develop the virtue of reverence. For if he focuses on virtue, then Heaven will bless him by continuing the Mandate.

'As king, he must ensure that the people do not behave badly, but he must also ensure that he does not use the death penalty unreasonably. If he rules well, then the virtue of good governance will be visible to all. If he does this, if his virtue is supreme, then throughout the land the ordinary folk will model themselves on him.

'Whether they are the highest or the lowest, everyone should have in common one concern, namely an ability to say, "We have received the Mandate of Heaven: may it last as long as it did for the Xia rather than for as short a time as it did for the Yin!"

'I hope that the way the king rules the ordinary people will show that he is worthy to have received the Mandate of Heaven.'

Kowtowing, Shao said:

'While I am but a simple minister, yet I am willing to rule over your troubled people. With all your officials and loyal people, we receive your Royal Decree which we will observe with due wisdom and virtue. I have no doubt that the king will receive the Mandate and as a result will become yet more glorious.

'There can be no question but that the king has indeed been given the Mandate of Heaven. This is why I stand here and offer both reverence and alongside this, veneration.'

The king here is King Cheng, the nephew of the Duke of Zhou and the young king mentioned before. This chapter seems to be recorded exchanges between the king and the Duke of Zhou regarding the new capital city.

41

THE SOLEMN ANNOUNCEMENT ABOUT LUO

'Most illustrious king,' the Duke of Zhou said, kowtowing. 'My dear son, I come before you to present my Report.

'It would not have been appropriate for you, the king, to appear to know the limits of Heaven's Mandate, nor its foundations. However, I as well as the Grand Protector have taken it upon myself to visit the Eastern Lands and to investigate them thoroughly to find a site for the new capital. I can now report that I have found a suitable site for the people's illustrious leader to settle.

'It was on the morning of the Yi Mao day when we came to the city of Luo and there I consulted the oracle to ask about the area of the River Li which lies to the north of the Yellow River. I then asked the oracle about the areas that lie to the east of the Jian River and to the west of the Chan. And all of the oracles favoured Luo as the site of choice. This favourable outcome was also the case when I consulted the oracle with regards to the east of the River Chan. They all favoured Luo, which is why this humble messenger brings you not only the map but also the oracles.'

The King kowtowed and replied:

'The Duke, who is always in awe of Heaven, has as a result

found where the new capital of the Zhou should be established. The Duke has come as a messenger to me, bringing the oracles in order that I might see for myself that they are auspicious. Let us now both work together. For the Duke has shown that this is good and that we shall be blessed by Heaven for untold generations to come. This is why on hearing these words I have kowtowed.'

The Duke replied:

'I recommend that you perform rituals in the Yin style at the dedication of the new city but that you drop all the ostentation they used to use. I will order all the heads of the main departments to come to join the King of Zhou and will give them their specific tasks.

'The King now needs to declare his will and he should order that those who are known for their merit will be the first to be chosen to perform the ritual sacrifices. Command them that they must assist you, because you have received the Mandate. By showing your merit and training your officers diligently, you will inspire everyone.

'Embrace them like friends so they will not plot but be like friends.

'Do not let them behave like a fire, which can be smouldering away and then suddenly, and for no apparent reason, can burst into flame. And once it gets going, it cannot be extinguished.

'Follow the proper rituals and activities which you already know. And encourage those who are in Zhou now to come up to the new capital and to work with the others. Encourage those who work hard and apply themselves intelligently. Be generous in your rewards. Build on the existing wealth of the country. This way, your name will be celebrated for generations to come.'

The Duke continued:

'While it is true that you are only young, it nevertheless falls to you to finish this task. For example, show respect to the princes who have come, but also observe who amongst the many brought tributes. And who did not.

'Likewise, far more will be discovered from watching the performance of the rituals than by just observing the tributes.

If there is no sincerity in the performance of the rituals, then we know that the offering of the tribute was also without sincerity. Such behaviour makes the people gossip that such rituals are of no importance and this only leads to discontent and rebellion.

'It is only natural that you depend upon me, my son. So follow my advice. Pay attention to what I will teach you and how I guide you in helping the people to behave properly.

'Let me be clear.

'If you do not do so at this time, then you cannot expect that the gift of the Mandate to you will last very long. If, however, you follow the ways of your upstanding father with true sincerity, and if you follow my advice, then you will not go astray. Nor will anyone go against your commands. So go now and undertake this with proper respect and reverence. Rule with kindness and with generosity and this will ensure that the people will look to you for protection.'

The King himself now spoke.

'Duke, your wisdom illuminates me, a mere youth. Even someone as young as I am can come to understand the wonders of King Wen and King Wu because of their virtue. By following the Mandate of Heaven we can unify the people, which will ensure peace for everyone across the whole of the country. As a consequence, I shall now honour people who are worthy. I will ensure that the rituals which will launch this will be undertaken not only with due care but without unnecessary show. It is because of the light of your virtue, Duke, which shines out from the highest places and down to the deepest across the land, that there is tranquillity and prosperity as there was under King Wen and King Wu. This is why I, as just a young man, can now attend to the proper daily rituals. My dear Duke, your Grace's merit has helped to steer me thus far. May it always continue.'

The King then said:

'Duke. This young man must now return to the duties that he inherited upon ascending the Throne, but I command that you stay here. While order has been restored across the country as a result of the rites, true veneration still needs to be established again. This means your great task is not yet complete.

Set an example to my officials and their hardworking officers by finishing the task and in that way protect the people who were in the care of Wen and Wu. Your example will inspire and help the whole country. I must leave; but you must stay.

'Your efforts, so worthy of note, are devoutly appreciated, but do not try to stop me. You have set before me a model of working tirelessly for the well-being of the people, a model which is vital to me. So long as you stick to it, then everyone throughout the country and for generations to come will benefit.'

The Duke of Zhou kowtowed. He replied:

'At your command, then, I will stay here. I will honour your command and do everything in my power to protect the people, care of whom your grandfather King Wen received as a Mandate, as did your father King Wu. I cannot think of a greater honour. Please come back regularly to see how things are progressing and to see that the people of Yin are doing well.

'Such attention to detail by a new ruler sets a good example to others and to those who will come to rule Zhou after you. The model of government which is established here, in this central spot of the new capital, will enable the whole country to be at ease. This will mean that Your Majesty will have completed the task set before you.

'Along with all your ministers, I, Dan, will try to further the accomplishments of our forebears and also set an example for future ministers of Zhou. In doing so, I will seek to contribute to your growing wisdom and further the example established by your virtuous ancestor, your grandfather Wen.'

Later on, messengers came from the King. They carried two casks of black millet-flavoured spirits and a message saying, 'Warn the people of Yin; take good care of yourself. This is for you to use in the illustrious ritual but also for you to enjoy as well.'

The Duke replied:

'It is not appropriate for me to enjoy this, so I have offered it instead to King Wen and King Wu. I have asked that they keep watch for us so that the dynasty is kept free from danger and sickness and so that it will last for ever through such virtue and that the people of Yin will live long and successful lives.'

Then, turning to the messengers the Duke said:

'We thank the King that he has sent you to Yin with his commands. If all goes well, then these inspired commands will inspire us for generations to come. This will mean my son will likewise be honoured for many generations to come.'

On the Wu Chen day, the king came to the new city and he performed the winter sacrifice, offering a red bull to both King Wen and King Wu. He commanded that Yi compose a prayer of supplication and he also announced that the Duke of Zhou would be remaining there.

Once the King had overseen the sacrifice of the bulls, he proceeded to the Great Hall and there poured out the libation. The King ordered the Duke of Zhou to stay and Yi recorded this solemn announcement. This all took place in the twelfth month.

As a result, for the next seven years the Duke of Zhou carried out the instructions of the Mandate which was first given to Kings Wen and Wu.

The king, speaking through the words of the Duke of Zhou, is far from pleased that, having spared the survivors of the dynasty of Shang and moved them to be under his supervision in the new capital, they are complaining.

42

THE MANY OFFICIALS

The rule of the Duke of Zhou in the new city of Luo began in the third month. He began by making an announcement to the many remaining officials of the Shang kingdom.

'The King himself addresses you, the many officials of the Yin. We can but mourn the many disasters which the Yin brought upon themselves. This happened because the Mandate of Heaven made this decree. Now we, the Princes of Zhou, have had the Mandate bestowed upon us as a consequence.

'Guided by the wisdom of Heaven, we must undertake the role that falls to kings in fulfilling the Mandate against Yin as decreed by the Ruler. Let me make myself quite clear to all of you. Our little country of Zhou did not set out to topple the Mandate of Yin. Heaven itself withdrew it in disgust at the wickedness of Yin. Heaven supported us, otherwise we would never have dreamed of seizing the Throne. And how did we know that the Ruler was opposed to you? Why, even the ordinary people could see it spotlighted by the light of Heaven!

'I have heard it said that the Ruler on High guides through kindness. The Xia failed to live up to this, which is why the Ruler sought to correct them. However they ignored the Ruler's wishes and became even more degenerate – descending into lewdness and idleness and even trying to justify this kind of bad behaviour. Heaven's patience ran out and it removed the Mandate and instead sent disasters upon them.

'So it was that the Mandate passed to Tang the Conqueror, who, as commanded, overthrew the Xia and then ruled the country with Heaven's support.

'From the reign of Tang the Conqueror to the Emperor Yi, all the rulers tried to live virtuously and to undertake the proper rituals. This anxiety not to offend Heaven meant they acted properly and the Yin were protected. The rulers of Yin took care to emulate, but not compete with, the kindness of Heaven.

'But now, it is no longer like that. The last king monumentally failed to live according to Heaven. Just as bad, he failed to try and emulate the ways of the Ancestor Kings of this once great House. Abandoning himself to outrageous behaviour, he wilfully ignored the laws of Heaven and the needs of the people themselves.

'So it was that the time came when the Ruler on High was no longer prepared to protect him and instead sent down terrible disasters. There comes a time when Heaven no longer helps those who fail to shine with virtue. Let us be clear, when a state falls, no matter how great or small, it does so for good reasons.

'You officials of Yin now know why the Ruler has blessed our Zhou kings. The Command was given – destroy Yin – and this we have done and Heaven has been informed. In all our dealings we have been straightforward and your Royal Family should follow our example. I have to tell you, you violated the laws and it was you who attacked us from your capital. When I reflect upon this, I can see clearly that Heaven has punished Yin because you went so spectacularly wrong.

'So now, listen to me, you load of officials.

'You are being sent to the West, but don't go thinking I am doing this just to upset you. This is happening because it is the Will of Heaven, so do not think of opposing me. I dare not delay.

'Do not think of holding this as a grudge against me. You will recall that it is recorded that the founders of Yin ousted the Xia. Yet you have the audacity to tell me that the officials of Xia were given posts in the Royal House alongside the other officials.

'Well, I am but a simple man who only pays attention to the virtuous ones whom I employ. None of you will be employed until I have sought guidance from the Heavenly Ones of the Shang as to what they wish me to do with you. Your current state has nothing to do with me. It is simply the Will of Heaven.

'The King has said that he wants you all to know the truth. That when I came here from Yen, I worked incredibly hard to try and lift the severity of the penalty that had been laid upon the rebellious people of the four countries. In fulfilment of the Mandate of Heaven, I have now punished you and have brought you here to be close to the loyal ministers so that you can learn how to be obedient too.

'Let me be quite clear and repeat to you all gathered here. I will not put you to death. That has never been my intention.

'Instead, this is what I command. I have built this great city of Luo to be a place where the whole country can find a focal point and where every prince can come to offer tribute and as the place where my ministers can serve. I invite you to settle here, as esteemed guests. You will retain all your lands, so you can afford to dwell here in honourable peace. Heaven will be kind to you if you show obedience and respect.

'But if you do not, then not only will you lose all your lands, but Heaven will exact revenge against you personally. Therefore, live here in this place and prosper and watch your families prosper year after year. This will happen because you decided to settle here. Do as I say because this arises out of genuine concern that you settle down happily here.'

43

BEWARE IDLENESS

The Duke of Zhou said:

> 'Indeed it is true that the wise man avoids idleness.
> He starts by understanding how hard farming is
> because from this comes the wealth
> and the wealth enables ease and idleness
> and so he understands how hard life is
> for the ordinary folk.
>
> Believe me, I have seen how hard things really are for the
>   ordinary people.
> While the parents labour hard in the fields,
> their sons have no appreciation for how much work there is
> and instead spend their time in idleness.
> They are rude and disobedient.
> So much so that they despise their parents, dismissing
>   them by saying: "These old people, hear nothing and
>   know nothing!"'

The Duke of Zhou said:

'I have indeed heard it said that the King of Yin, Tai Wu stood in trembling and fear of Heaven's Mandate and as a result was both respectful and reverent. Disciplined, he never indulged in idleness and ruled his people with reverent deference. As a result, he was able to rule his kingdom successfully for seventy-five years.

'Let us turn to his successor, Wu Ding. He laboured a long way from the luxuries of the Court, working side by side with the ordinary people. When his father died and he took the

Throne, he observed the three years of mourning and never spoke, not even once. Even when that formal period was over, he did not speak. When he did speak, what he said was of far greater significance as a result. Nor did he waste himself on pointless activities. So it was that he ruled over the state of Yin and at no time did anyone, high or low, complain. This is why Wu Ding ruled the kingdom successfully for fifty-nine years.

'If we look at his successor, Zu Jia, it never dawned on him to think of himself as a king, for he lived simply with the common folk. This is why, when he did come to the Throne, he knew only too well how important it was to have their support. As a result, he lovingly protected them and would never have dreamed of neglecting the weak and the defenceless, which is why Zu Jia ruled the kingdom successfully for thirty-three years.

'But from that time on, the kings of Yin lived lives of indolence.

'Born into idleness, they had no comprehension of the difficulties involved in farming, nor did they ever hear about the hardships of the ordinary people. Their only interests were their own selfish pleasures and ease, which is why none of them lasted for more than a few years – some up to seven or eight; some only five or six and some just a mere three or four years.'

The Duke of Zhou said:

'Indeed, now let us turn to our kings of Zhou such as King Tai and King Ji, for they ruled with reverence and compassion.

'King Wen dressed modestly and worked hard in the fields. He took particular care of the weak and defenceless and protected the people with kindness, cherishing them because he was an upstanding man. He was so concerned for the well-being of everyone that he often forgot to eat because he was working so tirelessly to care for them. Never in his wildest dreams did he consider his own pleasure, not even going hunting. As a result, he took the standard tributes but nothing more. Despite only receiving the Mandate of Heaven when he was middle-aged, he still managed to rule the kingdom successfully for fifty years.'

The Duke of Zhou said, 'Therefore, from this time forward, let all rulers follow his example.

'Avoid excess, idleness and sports such as hunting. This will mean that all that will be needed will be the basic tribute paid for by the mass of the people.

'Don't show yourself to be so full of yourself that you ever say: "Today I will do whatever I want." Neither the people nor Heaven will be impressed or approve of that. The danger is that they will imitate you and this will lead them into bad habits.

'So beware becoming like King Zhou of the Yin who through his debauchery and drunkenness lost all virtue.'

The Duke of Zhou said:

'I have heard it said that in the past, the wise ones would constantly correct, advise and encourage each other and as a result there was hardly any bragging or deceit to be found amongst the people. If you fail to listen to my advice, then your ministers will abuse their power, casting aside the codes of conduct that have come down from the Ancestor Kings. The outcome will be that the people, whether they are high and mighty or low and weak, will feel ignored and in their hearts and minds they will blame you. And so rebelliousness will arise, with some even going so far as to curse you openly.'

The Duke said:

'Remember. Those kings of old, the Yin kings Tai Wu, Wu Ding and Zu Jia, along with King Wen of our Zhou dynasty, all put their knowledge into practice. Whenever they heard that the common folk hated them and began to rebel, then they ensured that they turned to virtue again. They took full personal responsibility for any crisis. With such leadership, it is not surprising that the people moved on from their frustrations.

'Now, my concern is that if you do not listen to this but instead listen to those who will tell you lies, saying that the people are complaining and rebellious against you, you might act inappropriately. This will lead you to fail to reflect properly on your own role in all this and in your heart there will be no generosity. From this confusion you will act inappropriately, punishing the innocent and executing the harmless. If this fosters unrest, it will all be your fault.'

The Duke said, 'So, Your Majesty. Now that you have ascended the Throne, reflect on all this.'

Prince Shi is the brother of the Duke of Zhou and therefore uncle to the new king, Cheng.

44
PRINCE SHI

The Duke of Zhou addressed himself to Prince Shi.

'Heaven is without pity
and it has punished Yin.
As a result Yin has lost the Mandate.
This is why our dynasty of Zhou has received it.

'Will this be the case for ever?
I cannot say.

'Even with Heaven's help, it is impossible to determine whether the outcome will result in fortune or misfortune.

'Indeed, prince, you have said yourself that it depends upon us. But I cannot assume the blessing of the Ruler on High nor neglect the possibility of Heaven's wrath. Likewise, I do not count upon the support of the people.

'In the end all this depends upon us.

'We of your Household are only too aware that if in the future your descendants fail to show true respect to those Above as well as those Below, then this will spell the end of our dynasty.

'Heaven's Mandate is not easy to change nor easy to define. What I know is that the Mandate can be lost through lack of constancy, respect or the proper and wise use of virtue.

'Yet I, Dan, a simple man, cannot tell someone what to do. All I can do is remind him of the glory of his ancestors and encourage him to be like them. Heaven does not just expect us to hope all will be well. We must go forward by increasing the virtue and peacefulness of the king so that Heaven has no reason for withdrawing the Mandate which was given to King Wu.'

The Duke said:

'Prince Shi, I have heard of old that when Tang the Conqueror had received the Mandate he was assisted by Yi Yin as his minister and that this attracted the attention of the Emperor of Heaven.

'In similar fashion, King Tai Jia had his minister Bao Heng; King Tai Wu had his ministers Yi Zhi and Chen Hu. Because of the example they set, the Ruler on High was pleased. There was also Wu Xian, who managed the Household. King Zu Yi had Wu Xian and King Wu Ding had Gan Pan.

'The dynasty lasted for so long precisely because of the advice of these ministers, whose excellence meant that the government of Yin was protected. They did this through the proper use of ceremonial rituals, which pleased Heaven and so Heaven extended the Mandate. Everyone was a model of virtue, acting without regard for status and so everyone fulfilled their appointed duties. This in turn meant that the ruler ruled well and that simple man, wherever he sought the advice of the oracle, found that it confirmed his actions and their sincerity.'

The Duke then said:

'Prince Shi. Heaven favoured the just and wise and those who sustained and governed Yin accordingly. However, the last of their line reaped Heaven's wrath. Now you need to reflect on this so that the Mandate will remain with you and this will be achieved by you showing how wise this new state is in its management.

'When the Ruler on High punished Yin, he inspired King Wen to be virtuous and as a result he was given the Great Mandate. Because King Wen had many wise ministers, he was able to unite the country. Without having these wise and skilful ministers to guide him, the king's own virtue would never have been enough to reform the country. It was their comprehension of Heaven's authority which enabled these virtuous men to be such inspirational models. Through their guidance, they were able to enlighten King Wen. His understanding of how fortunate he was took him to the highest level. This was noted by the Ruler on High and this is why the Mandate was taken from Yin and given to him instead.

'Furthermore, because these ministers guided the king he achieved both success and contentment. Revering Heaven, they assisted the king and overcame his enemies, leading to his authority being respected throughout the land.

> 'Now I, Dan, a simple man,
> feel as if I am travelling down a mighty river.
> If we travel together
> we can cross this mighty river.
> Our current king is but a young man
> without experience.
> He needs our help
> but I cannot do this alone.
> If we do not work together
> to address his shortcomings,
> then no good will come of this.

'If we wish to hear the singing of the birds of good fortune and his praises to be sung, then we must pass on this ancient wisdom.'

The Duke then said:

'Indeed, Prince, reflect on this.

'The mandate you have received is not without its blessing but it also brings its own burdens as well.

'Therefore be generous, not for my sake but for the sake of your descendants. As you know, King Wu had confidence in you and taught you so that the people would be inspired by your example. He asked that you guide the king through your wisdom and caution. He urged that you must never ignore the virtue of King Wen and how he ruled.'

The Duke said:

'My Prince. I am sharing with you my most heartfelt deliberations in order that you, Shi, are protected. Reflect on how Yin was ruined and meditate upon the wrath of Heaven.

'You don't believe me?

'Well, all I am saying is that the future of our dynasty rests upon us two.

'Do you agree with me?

'Look. Heaven, seeing us working together, has blessed us, way beyond what we deserve. Pay attention to virtue and your wisdom will then enlighten the people and this will ensure the success of your lineage. Indeed, it is because you and I have been such faithful and devoted servants that we have been so contented to this day.

'So, shall we continue?

'Let us complete the worthy work of King Wen so that it spreads across the whole land, from the far oceans to where the sun rises. Then all will be in submission to you.

'My prince. Don't you agree that what I say makes sense?

'My only concern is the well-being of the people under Heaven. Indeed, my prince. You know the weakness in the virtues of the people.

> 'They mean well
> but it does not last.
> Knowing this,
> Carry out your duties
> But with due care.'

This again shows the concern of the new dynasty not to upset the Ancestors, even those of a rebel. His father was executed for his rebellion, but here the son, Zhong of Cai, also known as Hu, is given responsibilities including venerating his ancestors so that they will not be upset with the new dynasty.

45

THE INSTRUCTION TO ZHONG OF CAI

When the Duke of Zhou was the Prime Minister, in charge of all the key ministers and officers, the King's uncles spread malicious rumours about him. In particular, they criticized him for executing Prince Guan of Shang, exiling Prince Cai to Guo Lin with just seven chariots, and for dismissing Prince Huo from office for three years. Prince Cai's son, Zhong, was reverent and upstanding, so the Duke of Zhou appointed him to a senior post and when Zhou died, Zhong asked for a decree from the king granting him the region of Cai.

The King said:

'Hu, young man. You have reformed yourself and your virtue can be seen in how you behave. I therefore decree that you become the Prince of the Eastern Lands. Go there, respect us and show you can overcome the failings of your father through loyalty and piety to us. Do this and you will inspire your descendants through your example and remove the shame of the failures of your father through such dutiful actions. Model yourself on your grandfather, King Wen, and not on your treacherous father who so flagrantly disobeyed the king's commands.

'The Emperor of Heaven has no favourites
but only works through those who are virtuous.
The affections of the people
can be won through kindness.
Although not all acts of kindness are the same,
they do all contribute to good governance.
Likewise, not all acts of evil are the same,
but they all contribute to troubles.

'Pay as much attention to how you start something as to how you end it. Doing that will ensure that the end is not a failure. Failure to consider to what end you are working will mean that you will have an even greater disaster.

'Discipline yourself.
Be at peace with all on your borders;
support the Royal Court;
live in unity with all who work with you
pacifying and overseeing the common folk.
Find the Middle Path for yourself
and do not try to appear too clever or wise.
Do not ignore or dismiss the old rules
but reflect upon what you see and hear.

'Do not veer too radically in what you do about the rules. Do this and I, the simple man, will honour you.'

The king said, 'So, Hu, young chap. Go now and never ignore my commands.'

46

THE MANY PLACES

It was on the Ding Hai day in the fifth month that the King travelled from Yan to the city of Zhou. The Duke of Zhou announced:

'This is the word from the king.

"So! I make this announcement to the princes and officials from the four kingdoms and the many places.

"As you princes and people of Yin know, I have decided to pardon you. I should have decreed severe punishments for you all. You thought, and indeed you have behaved, as if you had Heaven's Mandate, but you failed to honour the rituals. The Ruler sent his wrath down upon the Xia, yet despite this, the last king of the Xia only sank deeper into idleness, failing to even consider the people. He sank so deep into mindless indulgence that he wasn't able to hear, even for one day, the advice of the Ruler. I know you know all about this. He counted upon retaining the Ruler's Mandate. Doing nothing to help the people, he instead brought greater woes upon the Xia. Through misrule there arose internal struggles, which left him incapable of guiding the people. On top of this there were some people from amongst the Xia whom he promoted despite their being known for their cruelty and this brought torment to the cities of the Xia.

"So Heaven decided to find a suitable lord for the people and gave the Mandate to Tang the Conqueror to destroy the Xia.

"Heaven did not leave the Mandate with Xia because there were others who were righteous in many other places and who had been turned away. Heaven also saw that the Xia officials were unable to care properly for the people. In fact, the officials encouraged each other in their abuses, leaving not a single official of any ability in control.

"Tang the Conqueror was successful because of the support of the many places which helped him overthrow the Xia, and so he become lord of all the people. Because he took care of their needs, they saw in him a model which encouraged them.

"From his time down to the reign of the Emperor Yi, all the rulers were illustrious and virtuous. They were careful in how they decided upon punishments and therefore provided a good example. Whether they were executing those charged with many crimes or granting freedom to those who had been falsely accused, what they did inspired others."

'Sadly, your ruler failed to maintain the Mandate of Heaven because he no longer had the support of the many regions. Indeed, the king has asked me to say the following: "I pronounce to the leaders of the many regions that Heaven had no plan to destroy the Xia nor for that matter the Yin either. It was entirely due to the disgraceful behaviour of your ruler. Thinking he had the support of the many regions and believing that he had Heaven's Mandate, he never once worried about his appalling behaviour.

"Heaven punished the Xia, replacing it with the Yin because of corruption and failure to observe the proper rituals.

"Then, in a similar way, your last Shang king did the same – indulging in excess and ruling without care or concern and so Heaven punished him too.

"The sage became a fool and the fool became, through reflection, a sage.

"For five years Heaven waited to see if this new king would reform and turn out to be a worthy ruler of the people. But he was not. So Heaven brought down its wrath upon the many regions to see if anyone would therefore arise who could be worthy of this role. But there was no one. The only ones found to be capable were our kings of Zhou, for they had taken proper care of the people and paid the proper respect to Heaven through the rituals. So it was that Heaven taught them, increased their worthiness and gave to them the Mandate that once was Yin's. This is why our princes now rule over the many places."

'Now, how come I am bold enough to say this?

'The only grounds I have for doing so is that I have been lenient in the way I have carried out the Commands upon the people throughout the land. Yet you here do not show me any gratitude for this in any way. Nor do you come forth to work with our King of Zhou and thereby share in the blessings of Heaven. You have been left with your lands and your homes, yet you still will not obey the king nor work to cultivate the blessings of Heaven.

'Instead, you follow the path of idleness, and you don't exhibit any love in your hearts even for your own well-being and you reject so violently the Will of Heaven. Your actions are illegal and yet you seek the support of honest folk!

'I have to warn you, respectfully. I have now had to arrest the worst offenders not just once, not just twice but in some cases three times. If you continue to ignore my kindness which has led me to spare your lives, I shall have no option but to inflict the most severe punishments. Including execution. This is not because we, the Zhou, wish to pursue a policy of oppressing you, but because your criminal activities leave us no other option.'

The king said:

'Indeed, you officials of the many places and you, the many officers of the Yin, you have had five years in which to carry out your responsibilities. You have rushed around, here and there, no matter whether you were senior or junior in your posts, all trying to do what you were told. The problems come because you do not understand the need for harmony – so try being harmonious yourselves. Your own families are torn apart – so start by practising harmony in your own homes. This way, the cities will be fine and all will be well.

'Try and avoid evil and instead fulfil your roles with reverence and care. Doing this will encourage trustworthy people to emerge to work alongside you. As a result, you will then be able to reside here in this city of Luo, to cultivate your lands, and Heaven will then show its favour and kindness to you. On top of this, we, the Zhou, will work with you, supporting and encouraging you in the Royal Court where we invite you to join us. This can only benefit you and mean that you will be ranked high amongst the officials.'

The king said:

'Indeed, all you officials. If you don't encourage each other to show proper respect for my Commands, then this dramatically highlights the fact that you will not pay proper respect to this Court. This encourages the people to ask why they should bother with the Court at all. If you turn against the Commands of the king through your being so lazy and perverse, then Heaven's wrath will descend on all regions and I myself will aid Heaven in this punishment and will exile you all far from here.'

The king said,

'I have no desire to issue these many proclamations, but I have to set my Commands before you.'

He added, 'This is the chance to start anew, but if you will not unite in this way now, then you can't complain to me in future about what happens to you.'

47

THE FOUNDATIONS OF GOVERNMENT

The Duke of Zhou said:

'Kowtowing at the announcement of the Son of Heaven, the king, we declare our loyalty. We, the officials of the king, his staff, officers, judges, Master of the Robes and of the army, have come to support you with our advice.'

The Duke of Zhou said:

'For Heaven's sake.
They all seem so keen
yet only a few know how anxious they really should be.

'This wariness was known by the ancient ones, even by those of the Xia when it was at its height. This is why they chose those who were able and who venerated the Ruler on High. Because such people valued knowledge and understood the nine virtues, they were willing to bravely confront their Prince, saying:

' "Kowtowing, oh Prince,
we wish to say that when,
as is your right,
you appoint people,
make sure you choose carefully for senior posts such as
    those with key legal and administrative responsibilities.
Don't just go by appearances,
thinking this one looks as if he is wise and virtuous
and then appointing him.
If you do this it is likely that all three senior posts will go
    to unworthy people."

'However, Jia failed to listen and those he chose were violent and because of this, he had no successors.

'Then there came Tang the Conqueror. During his reign he greatly enhanced the Mandate of the Ruler on High. He filled the three key posts with men of real talent, men known to be capable of the three levels of ability and who really were able to do this. Because Tang adhered to the strictest model of exemplary behaviour, these three officials themselves embodied the three levels of ability. Whether in the city itself or on the distant borders, unity was achieved and virtue was to be found.

'But when Zhou came to power, he embodied violence and those he chose exemplified aggression and oppression which they brought to bear on the affairs of state. He gathered people around him who saw indolence as a virtue, giving them government sinecures. This is why the Ruler resolved to punish him and why we were then given the Mandate that formerly was that of the Xia and had then been given to the Shang. This was in order that we might rule properly throughout the land.

'In consequence of this, both King Wen and King Wu fully understood the significance of the three key posts and the necessity of the three levels of ability. They therefore ensured that they appointed those who were engaged, heart and mind, in their labours. As a result, they reverently served the Ruler on High and held their offices for the good of the people. In carrying out these roles, they were assisted by worthy men at every level of government. This ranged from their personal households, through the legal staff to hundreds of others in minor positions or who were landowners. No matter what level they were at, all were good men.

'The princes themselves had ministers of education, of war and of Public Works who along with their assistants oversaw the minorities to east, south and west as well as the three administrative areas of the Yin.

'The appointments made by King Wen were of able and virtuous men because he could comprehend the hearts and minds of these men. Trusting them, he did not involve himself directly in their edicts and decisions as that was the role of these ministers and their assistants. Such issues of obedience and disobedience as they dealt with were their concern. Nor did he engage himself with law cases or regulations.

'After him came King Wu. He continued the policy of settlement, honouring the tradition of only appointing those who were virtuous and thoughtful. He did not disturb the established officers and their roles.

'Now indeed, you, young man, are the king. The foundation of your government will be based upon those whom you choose to appoint to the key posts. Make sure you really know these men before you offer them such powerful posts. Ensure they have the proper skills to control the government in order to help the people whose well-being has been entrusted to us. They must be able to harmonize all legal and regulatory practices and for this reason there must be no interference by you afterwards. So let us be careful of every utterance and every command, which is why we need to select those who are worthy. Then you can trust them to take care of the people whose well-being is ultimately your responsibility.

'Indeed, I, Dan, have received these teachings from others and I therefore pass them on to you, young man, you who now rule as king. From this time on, you must not engage with the administration of justice or the imposition of regulations. Follow the example of your great forebears and do not get involved. Leave that to those who have that responsibility.

'Throughout history, from the start of the Shang to the reign of King Wen of the Zhou, the foundation of government was based upon those who were appointed to have such responsibilities. Thus they were able to show they were able and worthy.

'No country can succeed in founding a government if it employs those who are false, speak ill or are without virtue. No future generations will thank you for that. So from now on, as you establish your government, do not appoint those who are false, who speak ill of others, but instead appoint worthy people. They will ensure that all goes well: well for the governing of your country and well for the Royal Family.

'Now, son of Wu, worthy grandson of Wen, you, my young man, are king, so do not interfere with the law courts. Leave all that to your appointees. Make sure that those you appoint to the military are good men. Then you will be like Yu the Great, extending your power throughout the land and over all below Heaven, reaching even to the seas themselves. This will lead to everyone acknowledging you as being in the mould of King Wen and reflecting the glory of King Wu. Maybe you will even be considered greater than them!

'Indeed, from now on, only appoint worthy men – so securing the foundation of your government.'

The Duke of Zhou then said:

'Grand Recorder, revered Su, Minister of Justice, carry out your duties with care so that Our Royal Kingdom's fortunes will grow from strength to strength. Following these models, always practise moderation when handing down punishments.'

The Duke of Zhou has at last managed to retire and here King Cheng takes up full responsibility.

48

THE OFFICIALS OF ZHOU

Seeking to unify the country, the King of Zhou toured the many estates of the nobles and punished those across the country who would not come to Court. Through this, he brought benefits to all the people. All six of the key nobles acknowledged the virtue of his rule and so he returned to the capital of Zhou to oversee the regulation of the offices of his government.

The king said:

'The wise ones in the olden days knew only too well that it is best to establish a government at times of stability and plan the protection of the country when there is no threat.

'Long, long ago, Yao and Shun appointed a hundred officials and made internal affairs the concern of the Chief Regulator, assisted by the Four Eminent Ones. External affairs were the concern of the administrators of the regions and the lead princes. As a result, all were united and all the myriad states were at peace.

'By the time of the Xia and Shang, the number of officials had doubled yet all was still well. These illustrious kings did not worry when founding their state about how many officials there were, but about whether they were of the highest quality.

'Now I, young as I am,
seek to respect virtue;
I concentrate day and night
on improving myself.
Because I admire these previous dynasties,
I not only try and model myself upon them
but also to teach you about them.

'This is why I have appointed the Grand Tutor, the Grand Instructor and the Grand Protector – the three dukes. They will now teach the way of direct management, of how to regulate yin and yang officials, not always rushing to fill such posts but waiting for the right time and person.

'The Deputy Tutor, the Deputy Instructor and the Deputy Protector are called the Three Alone, who work with the dukes. Their role is to implement changes and disseminate these throughout Heaven and Earth in order to help me, just a simple man.

'The First Minister is in charge of governing the state and has responsibility for the running of all other ministries throughout the land.

'The Minister of Instruction is responsible throughout the state for teaching about matters such as the Five Precepts* in order that the people might understand.

'The Minister of Rituals is responsible throughout the state for overseeing the ceremonies for the deities and humanity and for understanding their significance, no matter how great or small.

'The Minister of War is responsible throughout the state for overseeing the six military divisions and therefore the peace of the country.

'The Minister of Justice is responsible throughout the state for the punishment of the wicked and for handing down the sentences for those who are licentious and rebellious.

'The Minister of Works is responsible throughout the state for the four classes of the people and for overseeing the harvest.

'These six ministries with their diverse roles are also responsible for their assistants and for the direct oversight over the nine superintendents. Through this system, they can reach every person in the state.

'Every six years, the heads of the five tenures will report to the Court in person. At the end of the next six years, the king will make a progress and review how the historic regulations – which have been given to the four nobles who have such

---

* The Five Precepts were the five virtues of filial love; loyalty; marital fidelity; obedience; and sincerity.

responsibilities in each region – are being implemented. In turn, the nobles will review their assistants, helping everyone to fully appreciate the importance of their roles.

'Indeed,' the king said. 'Let all my officials and nobles take care to follow their duties and orders properly. Such orders must be acted upon immediately, not delayed or withdrawn.

> 'If you serve properly,
> then you can overcome ego
> and as a result the people will trust you.
> Look to the past
> to understand the duties you have today.
> Honour the traditions and the laws
> and then the government will not fall.

'Do what is laid down in the statutes of the state. Do not try to play with them using clever speeches, because casting doubts upon such things only leads to disturbance, and this in turn destroys good plans. If you are indolent, then neglect comes in its wake and this will destroy what is right. If you do not study this properly, you will be like someone facing a wall and you will not see that what you do is failing.

> 'Beware my nobles!
> Your goal should be merit.
> Your standing only increases through diligence.
> If you are determined in what you do
> then you can face the difficulties that will come in the
>   future.
> Watch out!
> High office can lead to pride;
> the benefits of office can lead to extravagance.
> Seek the virtue of unity
> by being respectful and reserved.
> Do not use your position to show off.
> Act with virtue
> and your heart and mind will then be at ease
> and day by day you will improve.

If instead you practise deceit,
then your heart and mind will be troubled;
and day by day you will make more and more mistakes.
Even when you are delighting in favour,
be aware that there are dangers
and so be cautious.
If you do not,
then disasters will arise.

'Promote the competent and encourage the officials to be as one. For when they are not all one, the government falls apart. You can take credit for your success if you have appointed good officials, but equally you must take responsibility for failure if you have appointed incapable officials.

'Indeed,' the king said. 'The three dukes are those whom you great officials must reverently serve, in order to make sure that there is no disorder in the running of the government. Do this and you will not only help your ruler but you will bring peace to the people and therefore there will be no discord anywhere in the land.'

Prince Chen is one of the sons of the now deceased Duke of Zhou. Here, he takes up some of his father's former responsibilities.

49

PRINCE CHEN

'Prince Chen,' said the king, 'I find that both filial duty and respect are united in you – and this is a virtue. You are filial and friendly to your older and young brothers and this makes me think you will display this in how you will rule the people. I therefore commission you to rule over the Eastern Borders and to show reverence to this commission. The people there remember only too well how the Duke of Zhou used to rule them as both teacher and protector and they honour him for this.

'Go, therefore, and with due care take up this responsibility. Follow his example and ways ensuring that the people are well governed.

'I have heard it said that good government, like a delightful scent, pleases the dear deities. And like incense, it is not the specific object offered but the worthiness of the supplicant which ensures this delightful scent.

'So become one with the ways of the Duke of Zhou and follow them day by day. Do not abuse this post in order to live in an extravagant way.

'Ordinary folk who have never met a sage before obviously have no idea what to expect and therefore when they do meet one they are none the wiser!

'Therefore be careful. You are like the wind and the people like the grass.

'Good government does not come easily.
Some things must change,
some things must remain.

'In planning whether to move forward or to stay still, listen to what the people say and if everyone is basically in agreement, then reflect on that. If you have a good idea, bring it first to the attention of the ruler in his Court. This will mean that when you are working it out later, you can honestly say that this is with the agreement of our ruler and in line with his virtue. Imagine how good things would be if every official acted like this.'

The king said:

'Prince Chen. Pay close attention to the model of the Duke of Zhou. Never use your power to extort nor to exploit through abuse of the laws.

'In your exercise of power
be gentle
but without seeming to be weak.
Look for those to serve
who in themselves embody harmony.

'If you find the people of Yin to be law-abiding, then when I say "punish them", do not unduly punish them. Likewise, when I say "forgive them", do not unduly forgive.

'Seek the middle path.

'Punish those who will not submit to your rule
or who ignore the regulations.
The ultimate goal of punishment
is of course the end of any need for punishment.

'But there are three types of crime which you must not
        spare,
no matter how insignificant the offence:
those who plot to overthrow;
those who incite rebellion;
those who challenge established traditions.

'Don't get upset by those who are foolish
nor expect everyone to be perfect.
Be patient
and you will be successful
for virtue comes with discernment.
Note those who do well
and you will encourage the less successful
to emulate them.

'Human nature at birth is good but this becomes distorted by the events of life.

'This leads them to oppose what those above them command because they want to follow their own desires. But if you follow the law and act virtuously, you can bring them back to the good and then they will rise so much higher. As a result, I, the simple man, will be very fortunate and your good services will be famous for generations to come.'

This is one of the most significant and detailed sections of the book, giving insights into the funereal rites of the Zhou. King Cheng is dying after reigning for thirty-seven years. It is around 1077 BC. The new king is King Zhao, who will become known later as King Kang – see chapter fifty-one.

50

THE AFFECTIONATE COMMAND

The king fell ill in the fourth month, when the moon was waning. On the Jia Zi day, the King washed his face and hands, put on his ceremonial robes and propped himself up on his jade bench. Then he called together all his officials. They all came, the Grand Protector, all the main lords, to the superintendents of the king's offices.

'Indeed,' the king then said. 'I am very ill, much worse than before and soon it will be time for me to go. The sickness gets worse day by day, without any reprieve. I am worried that soon I may not be able to express my intentions regarding my successor. This is why I will speak now. This is what I command you to do.

'Our forebears, King Wen and King Wu, ensured the well-being of everyone and through their glorious actions made sure all were properly instructed. Because of these actions, there was no opposition and the result was that they received the Great Mandate and took over from the Yin. Later, I, the insignificant one, with a due sense of awe received the Order from Heaven. And I have tried to follow the Great Example set by Wen and Wu, never daring to deviate.

'Now Heaven has struck me down with this illness and I fear

it will be fatal. So now I set out clearly before you what you must do. You must reverently protect my eldest son and heir, Ji Zhao. Help him through this difficult time.

> 'Make sure you assist those far off
> as well as those close at hand.
> Bring peace to all,
> throughout the state,
> great or small.

'I know how important it is that one conducts oneself with modesty and this is why Ji Zhao must be guided so he does not give way to rash emotions.'

The officials, having received their instructions, retired and took up their duties in the Court.

On the very next day, the king died.

Then the Grand Protector ordered Zhong Huan and Nan Gong Mao to follow the orders of the Prince of Qi, Lu Ji. The two men with their spears and with a hundred armed guards met Prince Ji Zhao outside the south gate and brought him in to one of the wings of the Palace as he was of course the chief mourner.

Two days later, he ordered that the rituals be performed and a full Record made.

On the seventh day after the death of the king, as the Lord of the West, he ordered the officials to provide wood and the necessary materials for the rituals.

He ordered the proper placement of the requisite screens. These were richly decorated with images of axes.

Three layers of bamboo mats with black and white silk fringes were placed facing south between the windows and doors. Tables decorated with jade inlays were placed upon the mats.

On the west side, facing east, other bamboo mats were spread out. These were richly decorated with pictures. Tables decorated with tortoise shell were placed upon the mats.

In the east, facing west, they placed fine mats made of grass with silk patterned borders. Tables decorated with jewels were placed upon the mats.

On the west side, facing south, were placed more richly decorated bamboo mats with black silk borders. Tables decorated with lacquer were placed upon the mats.

It was here that they displayed the Five Jewels alongside the many other treasures.

These included:

the Red Knife;
the Great Book of Instructions;
the Grand Jade Disc of Fortune
and the Sceptre of Power.

All these were displayed on the western side.
On the eastern side were displayed:

the Great Jewel;
the Jewels of the Foreigners;
the Heavenly Chime Stone
and the River Charts.

On the western side were also placed:

the Ceremonial Robes of the Yin;
the Great Tortoise Divination Shell
and the main drum.

On the eastern side were also placed:

the Spear of Dui;
the Bow of He
and the Bamboo Arrows of Chui.

The Grand Carriage was beside the Residency while the other three carriages were by the exit staircase, by the left exit and by the right exit.

Two men in leather caps held halberds, guarding the main gate into the palace. Four men in spotted deer-skin hats held their spears at the ready by either side of the two main staircases, to the east and west of the main hall. One man, dressed in official regalia and holding an axe, stood to the west of the main hall while another man in official regalia and holding a spear stood at the eastern end of the main hall. Holding a spear and also dressed in official regalia stood a man at the western end of the hall, while yet another officially dressed man holding a javelin stood by the main staircase.

The king, wearing a hemp cap and the brightly coloured regal robes, ascended the Residency staircase followed by the scholarly nobles and princes also wearing hemp caps with their black robes. Upon entering, they took their seats. The Grand Protector, the Grand Recorder and the Grand Master all wore hemp caps and bright red robes.

> The Grand Protector carried the Sceptre of Authority;
> the Grand Master carried the cup and the seal
> and together they ascended the staircase.
> The Grand Recorder brought the King the Record of the
>   Command.

He said:

'The noble Emperor, reclining upon the jade bench, set forth the Way as his last Command. He commanded you to follow him and continue to guide and rule the Empire of Zhou. Hold fast to the Great Mandate which unites all below Heaven. In this way show the yang light of Wen and Wu and their instructions.'

The king bowed twice and upon rising said:

> 'I am nothing,
> nobody,
> just a child.
> How can I rule the four corners of the land
> and assure reverence to Heaven's glory?'

He then received the cup and seal. Three times he filled the cup and three times he poured out the libations and three times he replaced the cup. The High Master said, 'It is accepted.'

The Grand Protector received the cup, descended and cleaned it and his hands and took another cup while holding his symbol of office and he repeated the libations. Passing the cup to another official, he bowed and the king acknowledged this and bowed in return. The Grand Protector received the cup and reverently offered it, sipping the offering, and then gave the cup to another official and bowed. The king bowed in return. The Grand Protector descended from the hall and the ritual objects were removed. The nobles then also left, passing through the temple gate beyond which they stood in readiness.

51

THE PROCLAMATION
OF KING KANG

The king came and stood inside the main gate while the Grand
Protector led out the princes of the west to the left of the gate
and the Duke of Bi led out the princes of the east to the right of
the gate. The bay horses with their red-coloured tails were
brought forth and those in attendance lifted high their sceptres
of authority and their gifts.

They said:

> 'We who are gathered here,
> we who are your officials,
> we bring you our gifts
> from the far-flung places
> of our homes
> to humbly lay them before you.'

They then kowtowed and the king, a model of virtue, bowed
in return.

The Grand Protector and the Earl of Rui, followed by everyone else, came forward, kowtowed and said:

> 'Son of Heaven,
> Imperial Heaven chose to take the Mandate
> from the imperial state of Shang
> giving it to Wen and Wu of the Zhou.

They proved they were worthy of receiving it
because they'd ruled the Western Lands so well.

The next king, following this example
both honoured and punished, as is fitting,
passing this example on to his descendants.

Now, your Majesty, practise caution
by increasing the Royal Army
and never again neglect the mandate
of your revered high ancestors!'

The king replied like this:

'Hear this, all you lords and noblemen.
I, being but a simple man, utter this proclamation.

Wen and Wu brought peace and good fortune.
Rather than overreacting to crimes
they responded to undue punishments.
They were truthful, and lit up
everyone around them under Heaven!
They had officers as brave as bears
and statesmen who were never two-faced
who protected and ordered the Royal House.

So they received the Mandate from the Heavenly Ruler.
Imperial Heaven guided them on their path
so they would rule the land well.
They appointed their leaders to govern,
and also protect the heirs to the throne.

So now, all my paternal uncles,
ensure you behave as well, and collectively
take on those tasks appointed to you
by your forebears in service of my Ancestral Kings!

Although you live long journeys away,
do not let your hearts and minds wander
far from the Royal Court!

Share my anxieties with me
and the duties that come with them
so that I, an orphan now,
will neither feel abandoned by you nor ashamed!'

All the dukes, having heard this proclamation, bowed to
each other and departed. The King took up his crown and once
again he put on the mourning robes.

52

THE COMMAND TO BI

Three days after the new moon, in the sixth month of the twelfth year of his reign, the King went on foot from the city of Zhou to the city of Feng. He was worried about the people of Cheng and issued orders to the Duke of Bi to protect and administer the eastern border.

The king said:

'Now, my paternal tutor, the Mandate of Heaven was received by King Wen and King Wu when they showed how virtuous they were to everyone. As a result, the Mandate was removed from the Yin. The Duke of Zhou served my Ancestor Kings well, and with them secured the Royal House. He subdued the rebellious Yin and banished them to the city of Luo. His plan was that by having them so close to the Royal Palace they would be reformed by his teachings. In just one generation – thirty-six years, to be precise – this worked. There was no more conflict in the land, and I, the single man, am at ease.'

The king said:

'Indeed, Grand Tutor, I now pass to you the duties of the Duke of Zhou and command you to go and discharge them. Make sure you distinguish between the honest citizen and the thug – taking into consideration their context and connections.

'Highlight the evil by emphasizing the good.

'Let it be known that those who disobey will have the boundaries of their land altered and let this instil fear in them, and thus a desire to conform. To make sure the country will remain at peace, secure the borders and strengthen the army bases.

'A government should be constant in what it does and its

instructions should be appropriate to the nature of the task in hand.

'Do not allow the exceptional to divert you from the ordinary. This is exactly what happened to the Shang. They delighted in flattery and valued those who were cunning above those who were wise. These traits are still prevalent today, so beware of them.

'I have heard it said that the aristocratic families who for generations have been favoured no longer feel the need to conform. They have as a result become indulgent and disregard virtue – even opposing the Way of Heaven. As a consequence, they set at naught what is good and mock what should be treasured and this bad example has influenced many generations.

'The officials of Yin had taken for granted this way of living and were so confident of their privileged position that they had lost sight of righteousness. They strutted their stuff in the face of others – and of course the end of all this was disaster. Yet still today, despite all that we have done to help their hearts and minds to reform, they are proving difficult to control. The hope is that through proper instruction, their power can be channelled to bring renewal which will shape many generations to come. If you are led by virtue and righteousness, then openness comes through following such great teaching. But if you will not follow these ancient teachings, then where else will you find wisdom?'

The king said:

'Indeed, Grand Tutor, the well-being of, or dangers for, the state depend on how the officials of Yin react. If they are not dealt with too severely or for too long a period, then it is possible that their virtue will improve.

'The Duke of Zhou always made sure he was well prepared before starting on any venture.

'Prince Chen always found the middle path in all that he did.

'You, Duke, can complete this in your actions, for you three statesmen, being united in heart and mind, have all found the True Way. Together, this True Way and the fact that the government is good for the people means that you can ensure double happiness for all.

'This will even affect the barbarian tribes from all four quarters – those very strange foreigners who, for example, button their coats on the left side – who will without exception trust me, the young child. So, you will build a reputation here in this city of Zhou, which will never fade – fame without end. Your descendants will be inspired to follow your example and will govern in a similar style.

'Listen!
You must not say
I cannot do this.
Instead commit yourself heart and mind.
Nor should you say
the people do not matter.
Pay attention to what you should do.
With due reverence take as your model the Ancestor
    Kings and as a result you will complete the excellent
    example set by your predecessors.'

We are now in the reign of King Mu, who traditionally reigned
between 1001 and 947 BC.

53

LORD YA

'Now, Lord Ya,' said the king. 'As you know, the loyal service
of your revered ancestors is written for all to see in the Great
Records. Generation after generation, they served the Royal
House with a true heart and their merit is justly recorded on
the great banner.

'I am but a child, yet I have inherited the duties and responsibilities from Wen, Wu, Cheng and Kang. I cannot help but
notice that the Ancestor Kings were assisted by their ministers
to control the whole land.

> 'I am so worried and disturbed.
> I feel as if I am treading on the tail of a tiger
> or walking on thin ice.
> This is why I now must command you to assist me;
> to become my arms and legs,
> my heart and my very spine.
> So go now,
> carry out your responsibilities
> and do not bring dishonour on your ancestors.
>
> Spread abroad the Five Precepts;
> These will unite the people.
> If you are straight with people
> then no one will dare not be.
> If you do not follow the Middle Way,
> then how can the hearts and minds of the people

be encouraged to do likewise?
The ordinary people,
they mumble and grumble through the summer heats and
    storms. But then they also do this in the winter as
    well – only this time complaining about the cold!
How hard life is.
Reflect upon their hardships
and therefore wish to ease their burdens.
Then the people will be at peace.

'Indeed, the programmes of King Wen were very good. Note
how well King Wu carried them forward. They inspire and
inform all of us who are their descendants because they are so
true and without fault. Follow them with reverence in order to
help me follow faithfully my ancestors. This will mean I am
worthy of both Wen and Wu and you will have obeyed the
commands of your own ancestors.'

The king added the following:

'Lord Ya. Follow the example and practices set by your
ancestors. Whether the government is good or bad for the
people hangs on this. So, follow the pattern set by your ancestors of how to govern and this will in turn glorify your ruler.'

This is also King Mu.

54
COMMAND TO QIONG

'Earl Qiong,' said the king, 'Unlike my forebears, I am not worthy to sit on the throne of the Prince. In fact, such a thought fills me with fear and trepidation.

'I wake up in the middle of the night, wrestling with my anxieties.

'Just think about it. Wen and Wu were illustrious and sagacious. Their statesmen, whether the highest or the lowest, prized integrity and goodness. In fact, all who served them were exemplary, being busy from morning to night with just one concern – to serve their ruler. Whether they were coming in or going out, standing or sitting, they showed nothing but respect. Whatever they decreed, it was for the good and as a result the ordinary people were reverent and everywhere there was contentment. I alone am unworthy. I must rely on my assistants to correct my faults and to confront my errors. In this way I will be able to overcome the falseness of my heart and be able to be worthy of my ancestors.

'Now I command you to act as the Grand Judge and to ensure that all those who serve me behave properly. This will then mean they can help their prince to be more virtuous and so I will be able to overcome my failings.

'But take care in the choice of assistants.
Do not choose those who flatter
or who at first sight seem to be good.
Avoid sycophants

and choose only those
who have a good reputation.
For when those who serve are true,
the prince will be true also.
But when those who serve are flatterers,
well . . .
the prince will think he is some kind of a sage!

'A prince's virtue depends upon his statesmen. And conversely, any lack of virtue also depends upon the statesman. Do not trust the obsequious, who will fill your ears and eyes with nonsense, nor trust those who twist the regulations of the Ancestor Kings. If you select officers, not because they are good but because they bribe you, they will eventually prove to be worse than useless. They will show no respect for the ruler and then I will lay all the blame for this on you.'

'Indeed,' the king said. 'Be respectful. Help the prince and thereby ensure law and order.'

55

THE PENAL CODES AND THE PRINCE OF LU

When the king was old and tired, he prepared the Order to Lu – codes of penal laws designed to ensure that the people throughout the land would obey them.

The king commanded:

'The ancient stories tell us that the first person to launch a rebellion was Chi You, chief of the Miao people, and that this had a deep impact on all the ordinary people. Encouraged by this rebellion, they without exception turned to thieving and murder, and like birds of prey they attacked the righteous. They turned into traitors and thugs and were piratical and violent.

'In response, the Miao people reacted with punishments, not with gentleness, and they created the Five Punishments. These were so severe that they called them "laws" and this resulted in innocent people being killed, having their noses and ears cut off, being castrated and branded. Regardless of what you might or might not have done, these punishments were applied, no matter what the circumstance. This deeply affected the people, who became depressed and confused, unable to do any good or trust anyone. They no longer honoured vows or promises. The result of this terror was that eventually they could stand it no longer and they sent their protests on High. This led to the Ruler on High investigating what was going on with the people, but he could find no trace of virtue. Instead, there was the stench of cruelty.

'The Imperial Ruler was moved to pity by the sufferings of the innocent masses who were being killed. In response, he brought down his wrath upon the Miao tribe. Initially he curbed them, but ended by wiping out the entire tribe so that they would have no succeeding generations. They were exterminated for ever.

'He then ordered Chong and Li to sunder for ever the links between Earth and Heaven in order to make clear the separate roles of each and to end the engagement with the spirits.

'Those in positions of power at every level worked together to highlight the proper principles of duty. For example, that the helpless, such as widows, were no longer to be neglected or disregarded.

'The Imperial Ruler listened to what the ordinary people, the helpless and the poor, had to say about the behaviour of the Miao. Awe and terror arose from his display of virtue, which also served to illuminate and enlighten them all. The well-being of the people was given as a charge to the Three Princes to test their sincerity.

'Lord Yi worked on the rites and on their dissemination in order to enforce properly respectful behaviour.

'Yu was ordered to control the waters and the land and to make a record of all the mountains and rivers.

'Qi was ordered to promulgate the spread of the knowledge of agriculture so the people could produce good harvests.

'The end result of the labours of the Three Princes was that all went well with the people.

'The Minister of Justice ensured that all the communities understood the appropriate punishments to be given according to the laws and the teachings, and through this they were able to demonstrate virtue. With solemn reverence to Above and such a shining example to Below, the whole world was enlightened. The moderate use of punishments encouraged the growth of virtue. Through this, the people accepted the role of government and its obligations. This had the effect of enabling the magistrates to act not just against the powerful but against the rich as well and as a result there was true respect and caution. No inappropriate words were spoken nor needed. In such times, the virtue of Heaven naturally arises from the original Mandate, earning the respect of those below.'

The king said:

'Oh, you leaders and rulers from across the land. You who judge and decide, take the Shepherd of Heaven as your model. You should also take as your example Bo Yi with his strict enforcement. You should learn from the failures of the Miao, who did not exercise either strict or proper enforcement. They also failed to appoint good officials to oversee the proper implementation of the Five Punishments. Instead, they appointed the vicious and the corrupt who used the Five Punishments to confuse others. Eventually the Ruler on High could forbear no longer and decided to destroy the Miao utterly. As the Miao were unable to exonerate themselves, they were wiped out and there are no descendants to this day.'

The king said:

'Indeed, bear this disaster in mind, my people, and pay attention to what I say, for this is my Command. From this day on, be careful and avoid indulgence. Today Heaven has given us the authority to make proper use of punishments. Therefore distinguish between habitual and initial offenders.

> 'With care fulfil Heaven's Will
> and work with me alone.
> If I think I must be absolute,
> you do not have to be;
> when I think I must be lenient,
> you do not have to be.

'Use the Five Punishments with due care and with awe in order to enhance the Three Virtues. As a result, I, a simple man, will ensure contentment and the people will be secure, as will be the stability of the country.'

The king said:

'Oh, come now, you leaders and rulers. I will tell you how to apportion punishments. Because there is nothing more important than the penal codes, you must appoint those who are

worthy and that will instil respect for the codes, as people will
see that justice is done throughout the land.

> 'When both parties are present and ready,
> the judge should listen to the Five Charges.
> If the Five Charges lead to the Five Punishments,
> then so be it.
> If however they do not justify them,
> then don't use the Five Punishments.
> Instead use the lesser ones,
> the Five Penalties.
> If even these are too severe,
> then use the Five Faults.
> If you use the Five Faults
> beware of abusing your authority;
> beware of vengeance;
> prostitutes;
> bribery
> and undue pressure or lobbying.

'Make the punishment fit the crime.

'Judge carefully and equitably.

'For example:

'If there is uncertainty about imposing any of the Five Punishments, then be lenient.

'When there is uncertainty about imposing any of the Five
Faults, then be moderate.

'In all cases, give them full and proper attention. Check all
the details with as wide a range of individuals as possible and
only then make a decision. Discuss the case thoroughly. Without proper evidence, no decision should be made, so dismiss
the case. In every case, be aware of the Majesty of Heaven.

'If you are uncertain whether to brand someone, commute
this to a fine of six hundred ounces of copper – but only when
you are sure.

'If in doubt about a nose slitting, commute to twice that, but
only once you are sure.

'If in doubt about a foot amputation, commute this to three thousand ounces of copper, but only once you are sure.

'If in doubt about castration, commute this to three thousand, six hundred ounces of copper, but only once you are sure.

'If in doubt about execution, commute this to six thousand ounces of copper, but only once you are sure.

'The types of crimes for which fines exist are as follows:

> Face branding 1000;
> Nose slitting 1000;
> Foot amputation 500;
> Castration 300;
> Execution 200.

'Therefore, of the Five Punishments there are 3,000 cases which are commutable.

> 'Do not confuse major and minor offences;
> do not allow complications to arise
> and ignore outmoded laws;
> investigate;
> work within the law;
> make a judgement accordingly
> and you will show you are equal to the task.

'If appropriate, downgrade a punishment. Likewise, if it is appropriate, upgrade a punishment. Depending upon the circumstances, balance the use of a major or minor punishment. Different generations require more severe or less severe levels of punishment.

'Although not literally deadly, nevertheless the impact of fines can be almost as deadly in their emotional impact.

'This is why only people of proven worth should be involved in legal affairs, because they can be trusted to make proper decisions, rather than facile and false ones. Before you proceed, check that the right decision has been made. When using the Book of Penal Codes, show compassion and reverence, so that this encourages everyone to reflect properly. This way, your decisions will strike a proper balance regardless of whether it is a punishment or a fine. If you do this, then at the end of the case all parties will feel justice has been served. Write up the reports fully. If there are two offences, treat them as two separate offences.'

The king said:

'Indeed, all you leaders and members of my family, treat all this with due reverence. I speak with due reserve. I stand in awe before proper punishments because they assist virtue. Now Heaven cares for the people and so has appointed us to represent it here below. Therefore display wisdom in how you deal with charges. Listen to both sides, and then make a decision to ensure law and order. Do not let one side put pressure on you through special pleading. To accept bribes is to make your decisions valueless because they are a manifestation of wrongdoing and will generate evil. Always be acutely aware of the wrath of Heaven.

'Remember, it is not Heaven that fails to act dispassionately: it is humanity that does so and brings disaster upon itself by ignoring the Will of Heaven. The danger is that if people believe that Heaven itself is not just, then they will not trust any government which operates under Heaven's aegis.'

The king said:

'Now, every one of you gathered here needs to look to the example of virtue to understand how to care for the people. If you are wise, you will listen to me. These laws are the fruits of the wisdom of the past and have decreed appropriate punishments for all offences, related to the Five Perfections. Administer justice with due care and concern and in doing so you will help to re-establish a state of harmony. The harmony that you received from your forebears.'

The year is now traditionally 770 BC and a new king, Ping, has risen from the ashes of the disastrous reign of King Yu (781–70 BC), who, like the final kings of the Xia and Shang, had become decadent and whose kingdom was overrun and its capital sacked. The new king is addressing Lord Wen (here also referred to as Yi He), one of the nobles who came to the rescue of the failing dynasty after the invaders were resisted, though the old capital was never captured. From now on, the dynasty is known as the Western Zhou.

56

THE COMMAND TO PRINCE WEN

The king said as follows:

'Uncle Yi He. How very wise were Wen and Wu and how brightly their virtue shone. It illuminated on high and was praised here below and as a result, the Ruler on High bestowed the Mandate upon King Wen. He was assisted by your ancestors who were his ministers and they skilfully aided the ruler in not just the great affairs of state but also the minor ones as well. It was for this reason that our revered ancestors sat securely upon their throne.

'Sadly, it is now I who have inherited the throne. And I am but a shallow youth. As a result, Heaven has now sent down terrible punishments, making it impossible for me to take proper care of the common people. Our kingdom has been invaded and among the family of my advisors there is no one with any real experience from which they can offer me advice.

'As for me, well, I'm not capable either. Do you see why – oh, my ancestors, my forebears – why I am so worried? I, a man alone, need help if I am to reign in peace.

'Uncle Yi He, through you the glory of our illustrious ancestor shines. It is like the example of Wen and Wu, so please bring all this together and ensure the well-being of your ruler. Your example of filial piety harks back to your illustrious ancestor, which is why you have been there for me, coming to my aid in times of trouble. This is why I continue to admire you so greatly.'

The king said:

'Uncle Yi He.
Go back to your home;
inspect your troops;
secure your lands.
I award you a jar of black millet spirit,
deliciously flavoured;
a red bow with a hundred red arrows;
and four horses.
Go back home, my Uncle,
reassuring those who live both near and far.
Take care of the ordinary people
and do not seek a life of ease.
Show compassion for all in your jurisdiction
and this will bring to fruition your own virtue.'

The Duke here is the son of the famous Duke of Zhou. The king is King Cheng and while the date is uncertain it is probably in the second half of the eleventh century BC. Its being placed here makes no particular sense. It does reflect the somewhat confused nature of the Shang Shu, *not surprising given its very complex history. See the Introduction, pages l–lviii.*

57
THE OATH AT BI

The Duke said:

'Oh listen to me, my people.
Shut up and hear my Command.

We are about to set out to punish the tribes in the Xia
         and Huai area because they have rebelled.
Gird yourselves in your armour,
take up your weapons
and don't even think about not being ready.
String your bows;
sharpen your lances and spears;
prepare your swords –
and don't even think about not being prepared.

'Now we will free the oxen and horses, no longer keeping them penned up. Put away your traps and pits you use for hunting, for none of these creatures must suffer harm. If any do, you will suffer the appropriate punishment. If any horses or oxen or, come to that, servants of yours – whether male or female – run off, don't rush off after them. Ensure later that they return. You will be compensated by me. If you do dare to break ranks and chase after them, and then fail to catch them, you will be punished accordingly. Do not let anyone steal; don't allow anyone to jump fences and walls to seize stray horses, oxen or servants. If you do, you will be punished accordingly.

'On the Jia Xu day, we will set off to punish the Xu tribe, so prepare food for the march. Any failure to do so will be severely punished. You men from the three territories and the three regions, prepare the raw materials, for we will start to build the fortifications this very day. Failure to do so will bring severe punishments – possibly even death. You men from Lu, from the three territories and the three regions, ensure there is adequate fodder, because if you do not ensure that there is plenty, you will suffer the most severe punishments.'

The events here take place during the reign of King Ping. Rebellion and inter-kingdom warfare is now the norm. The duke here is the Duke of Qin, who has come to meet his defeated army commanders. Expecting to be put to death, they instead hear the duke take responsibility for their military defeat himself in what has become the classic example of a ruler taking responsibility for the actions of those under him. A model Confucian. This is sometimes thought to have taken place during the reign of King Xiang – 651 to 619 BC.

58
THE OATH AT QIN

The Duke said:

'Officers, listen to me. Be quiet now.
I'm going to make an important announcement.

The old ones had a saying, you know
*"The people always prefer an easy way of life.
It's easy to criticize them for this, but hard to do so
without some degree of hypocrisy!"*

It saddens me that the days and months go by
and they will never come again.

I didn't listen to those old advisors who criticized me,
I preferred the company of my young friends.
But now I realize I need the insights of their grey heads
because that will stop me making a mess of things.
How I appreciate those old men now,
even though they're weakened by age!

As for the young bucks who delight in hunting and riding
I haven't got time for them now.

And as for the superficial charmers who turn
a true man from the Way
I neither need them,
nor does the Emperor.

I have thought about all this and come to a decision.
One true minister, pure and simple, without
any other qualities but a heart and mind at rest
– appreciative of others as if their skills were his –
this is what I need above everything.

A man who, when he encounters wise men,
appreciates them with all his heart, more than he can say.
A man like this will care for my heirs and people
bringing great things to them all.

Compare this with a man who is jealous
of people more skilful than himself.
He seethes with resentment against them
when he finds out how wise they are;
then he blocks them, opposing their advancement!

Such a man will never protect my heirs or my people!
Hear me, a man like this is truly dangerous.

A state can be brought down by just one man.
It can also rise to glory, because of one man.'

Personalities of the Book

Chapter numbers in which these characters appear are given at the end of each entry.

Bao Heng. Minister to King Tai Jia (ancestral king of Shang). 44

Bi, Duke of. Royal official of King Cheng and King Kang. Sent to administer the Eastern border. 51, 52

Cai, Prince. Exiled to Guo Lin with just seven chariots. 45

Chen, Prince. Son of the Duke of Zhou, who takes up some of his father's duties. 49, 52

Chen Hu. Minister of King Tai Wu, one of the three Ancestor Kings of the Zhou. 44

Cheng, King of Zhou. Successor to his father King Wu and nephew of the Duke of Zhou. Reigned from 1115 to 1078 BC. 34, 35, 36, 38, 39, 41, 42, 45, 46, 48, 49, 50

Chi You. Ancient leader of the Miao people and the first person known to have launched a rebellion. 55

Chong. With Li, sundered for ever the links between Earth and Heaven. 55

Chui. Minister for Works under Emperor Shun. 2

Dan: *see* the Duke of Zhou

Fa: another name for Wu, the first ruler of the Zhou Dynasty.

Feng: *see* Kang, Prince

Gan Pan. Minister to King Wu Ding. 23, 44

Gaoyao. Minister for Justice under Emperor Shun and a model of the just Confucian official. 2, 3, 45

Gaozong, King of Yin. Successor to Zhong Zong. As a model king he is supposed to have reigned for fifty-nine years. 24

Ge. A petty ruler who pleaded poverty as the reason why he could not make sacrifices. Tang ordered his own people to help him, but Ge murdered them as they brought the sacrifice materials for Ge. Tang therefore overthrew Ge c.1781 BC. 11

Guan, Prince of Shang. A rebel executed for his rebellion against the new Zhou dynasty. 45

Guanshu. One of the ten sons of King Wen, brother to the king, uncle to the young king, and brother to the Duke of Zhou. 34

Gui. Last king of the Xia dynasty, who came to the throne in 1818 and was overthrown by Tang the Conqueror in 1766 BC. He was one of the archetypal bad rulers of Chinese history. 10, 11

Gun. The first person appointed by Yao to try to tackle the Great Flood, even though Yao knows him as a rebel, but he doesn't understand enough and after nine years fails. In the Book of Zhou, chapter thirty-two, he is referred to as having failed to respect the Divine Order. 1, 32

He. An official, always appears with Ho. 1, 9

Ho. An official, always appears with He. Both are charged by Emperor Yao with responsibility for the agricultural calendar, a symbol of the partnership between the Emperor and Heaven in maintaining order and the balance of nature. It seems that these names later became official titles for those responsible for the astrological calculations and calendar. 1, 9

Hu: *see* Zhong, Prince. 45

Huo, Prince. Dismissed from office. 45

Ji, King. Together with Wen and Tai, one of the three Ancestor Kings of Zhou. 43

Ji Zhao. Son of King Cheng, later King Zhao and also known as King Kang. Reigned from 1078 to 1052 BC. 50, 51

Jie. Son of Yu and second ruler of the Xia Dynasty, he reigned from 2197 to 2188 BC. Chapter seven relates to a rebellion against him around 2193 BC. 28

Kang, Prince. Ninth son of King Wen, also called Feng. Brother to Guanshu and the Duke of Zhou. 37, 38, 39

Kang, King: *see* King Zhao

King of Xia: *see* Gui

Kui. Minister for Music and Poetry under Emperor Shun. 2, 5

Li. With Zhong, sundered the links between Earth and Heaven. 55

Liu. Noble. Remembered from the past as one of the founders of the Zhou House, building on the worthiness of the Great King. 31

Long. Minister for Information under Emperor Shun. 2

Lu Ji, Prince of Qi. 50

Mu, King. Reigned between 1001 and 947 BC. 53, 54
(976–922/ 956–917)

Nan Gong Mao. Court official of King Cheng. 50

Pang Geng. King of Shang Dynasty, who reigned from 1401 to 1374 BC. He is the subject of chapters eighteen to twenty which tell of his moving the capital to Yin and this is when the name of the dynasty changes. 18, 19, 20

Ping, King. Followed King Yu, 770 BC. 56

Prince Yin. Same person as Yi: *see* below.

Qi. Minister for Agriculture under Emperor Shun. 2, 5, 55

Qi, King. Built up the Royal House. 31

Qi, Viscount of. The same person as the Viscount of Wei. He refused to run away when the Shang dynasty fell and was honoured by King Wu of the Zhou for his integrity. He is brought to lay out the Great Plan and then in chapter thirty-six he is given responsibility for the ancestor rituals for the Shang ancestors. 32

Qin, Duke of. He goes to meet defeated army commanders, and acts as a model of Confucian responsibility as a leader; not putting them to death but taking responsibility himself. Thought to refer to an event in the reign of King Ping, *c.*750 BC, though other traditions place it *c.*628 BC. 58

Qiong, Earl. High Chamberlain under King Mu. 54

Rui, Earl of. Royal official of Kings Cheng and Kang. 51

Shao. Grand Protector. Believed to be one of King Wen's ten sons, and with responsibility of helping his brother, the Duke of Zhou, find a site for the new capital. 40

Shi, Prince. Another of the brothers of the Duke of Zhou and with him the key guardian of the young King. 44

Shu, King. Laid the foundations of the Zhou. 31

Shun. He was a model of correct behaviour despite having a terrible father, stepmother and brother. He is recommended to the Emperor Yao for his temperance and ability to build harmony in difficult circumstances. Chosen by Yao to succeed him. He is the last ruler in the Age of the Five Rulers. Traditionally ruled from 2255 to 2205 BC. 1, 2, 35

Su. Grand Recorder, Minister of Justice. 47

Tai, also **Tai Wu**. Together with Ji and Wen, one of the three Ancestor Kings of Zhou. 43

Tai Gang. The third Xia ruler. Reigned from 2188 to his overthrow in 2159 BC, recorded in chapter eight, where his five brothers lament his foolishness which leads to his fall. 8

Tai Wu. Shang king before Wu Ding. 43, 44

Tai Jia. Second ruler of the Shang, who reigned from 1753 to 1700 BC. He is the subject of chapters 14–16, 44.

Tang the Conqueror. First ruler of the Shang (later called Yin) Dynasty. He conquered the corrupt Xia dynasty and received the Mandate of Heaven to rule. His reign was from 1766 to 1753 BC. 10 onwards.

Tang of Dao: another name for Emperor Yao, because he was also the ruler of Dao and Qi.

Two Dukes. Brothers to the King and to the Duke of Zhou, Prince Kang and Guanshu. 34

Wei, Viscount of. Outspoken minister of the last Shang/Yin ruler, Zhou. First mentioned in chapter twenty-six, he reappears in chapter thirty-six and is honoured as having taken a principled stance against the corruption of the last ruler, Zhou. He is appointed to oversee the rites honouring the Shang ancestors under the new Zhou dynasty. 26, 36

Wen. King and Lord of the West and ruler of the state of Zhou, who conquers the land of Li in chapter twenty-five and begins the downfall of Zhou, the last and most despised ruler of the Shang/Yin dynasty. Mentioned from 25 onwards.

Wu. First ruler of the Zhou dynasty and son of Wen. He finished the overthrow of the Shang/Yin dynasty and ruled from 1122 to 1115 BC. He is also called Fa. 27 onwards

Wu Ding, King. Laboured alongside ordinary people before ascending the throne, which he held from 1324 to 1264 BC. He mourned his father's death by not speaking for three years and rarely spoke thereafter. 21–3, 43, 44.

Wu Xian. Managed the Household of King Tai Wu, one of the three Ancestor Kings of Zhou, and was also Minister to King Zu Yi. 44

Xie. Minister for Education under **Emperor Shun**. 2

Ya, Lord. Official under King Mu. 53

Yao, Emperor. The penultimate ruler of the group know as the Five Rulers, he is a semi-mythological figure credited with having first defined the calendar and its practical use, especially for the purposes of agriculture. He has at least four brothers. His son, the Crown Prince, is dissolute, so he needs to find another heir. He has at least two daughters whom he is willing to send for a strategic marriage with Shun, whom he ultimately chooses to succeed him. Traditionally ruled from 2357 to 2255 BC. 1

Yi. Prime Minister of Tang, who in the chapter bearing his name (chapter thirteen) is addressing the successor to Tang, King Tai Jia, who reigned from 1753 to 1700 BC. 13, 14–17, 44

Yi, Lord. In charge of the Temple of the Ancestors, under Emperor Shun. 2, 3, 55.

Yi, Emperor. Penultimate ruler of the Shang and father of the last ruler, Zhou. Reigned 1191 to 1154 BC. Seen as the last virtuous ruler of the Shang. 38 onwards

Yi, King. Ruler of Jiong. Also known as Yi the Great or Yi the Archer. One of the great semi-mythological figures of China, he is credited with shooting eight false suns out of the sky and thereby saving the world from destruction by drought. The counterpart to the story of the Great Flood. He opposed the corrupt Xia ruler Dai Gong and overthrew him. 8

Yi He. Uncle to King Ping. 56

Yi Yin: same person as Yi, see above

Yi Zhi. Minister of King Tai Wu, one of the three Ancestor Kings of the Zhou. 44

Yu, also called **Yu the Great.** Prime Minister under Emperor Shun, having quelled the Great Flood after ten years of devoted service. He is chosen to succeed Shun and is the founder of the Xia Dynasty. He rules from 2205 to 2197 BC. One of the great heroic figures of Chinese history and mythology. 2, 3 onwards

Yue. Prime Minister to King Wu Ding of the Shang Dynasty (by then renamed the Yin Dynasty), who reigned from 1324 to 1265 BC. Also called Fu. First appears in chapter 21.

Yu Shun: *see* Shun

Zhao, King. Takes over from his father, King Cheng. Also called King Kang. 50, 51 (and Ji Zhou 50)

Zhidan. One of the sons of Yao, who lost his chance of ruling because of his bad behaviour. 5

Zhong, Prince. Son of Prince Cai, a reverent man promoted by the Duke of Zhou and inheritor of Cai. Also called Hu. 45

Zhonghui. Advisor to Tang the Conqueror and the key speaker in chapter 11.

Zhong Huan. Court official of King Cheng. 50

Zhong Kang. Fourth ruler of the Xia, he reigned from 2159 to 2146 BC. 9

Zhong Zong. Early King of Yin. As a model king, he is reputed to have ruled for seventy-five years. 43

Zhou. The last Shang King, reigned from 1154 to 1122 BC. He is the epitome of the evil ruler, renowned for his cruelty and dissolute lifestyle. He is overthrown by Wu, the first ruler of the Zhou dynasty. 27 onwards, but is also the king referred to in 25 and 26.

Zhou, Duke of, also called **Dan.** The fourth son of King Wen, brother to King Wu of Zhou, to the 'Two Dukes', to Prince Kang (also called Feng), to the plotting Guangshu, and uncle to the young king who succeeds his brother. Zhou is the ultimate model Confucian official and was revered throughout the imperial history of China for his wisdom and sage guidance. 34 onwards

Zu Jia. King of Yin, successor to Gaozong, and as a model king ruled for thirty-three years. 24, 43

Zu Yi. Advisor to King Zhou of the Shang. 25